HERBS AND SPICES

The American Horticultural Society
Illustrated Encyclopedia of Gardening

HERBS AND SPICES

The American Horticultural Society
Mount Vernon, Virginia

For The American Horticultural Society

President
Dr. Gilbert S. Daniels

Technical Advisory Committee
Everett Conklin
Mary Stuart Maury
Dr. John A. Wott

Herbs and Spices Staff for The Franklin Library/Ortho Books

Editorial Director
Min S. Yee

Supervisory Editor
Lewis P. Lewis

Editor
Ken Burke

Art Directors
John Williams
Barbara Ziller

Creative Director
Michael Mendelsohn

Assistant Creative Director
Clint Anglin

Written by
James K. McNair

Contributing Writer
Rex Wolf

Illustrations by
Ellen Blonder
Cyndie Clark-Huegel

Production Director
Robert Laffler

Production Manager
Renee Guilmette

Production Assistant
Paula Green

For Ortho Books

Publisher
Robert L. Iacopi

For The Franklin Library

Publisher
Joseph Sloves

The cover photograph shows one of the satisfying results of herb gardening: tarragon, dill, yarrow, and sage being dried for future use. Photograph © 1982 by Walter Chandoha.

Hand cream recipe, page 89, reprinted by permission of Panjandrum/Aris Books from *Kitchen Cosmetics* by Jeanne Rose (1978).

Major Photography
Tom Tracy

Additional Photography
(Names of photographers in alphabetical order are followed by page numbers on which their work appears. R = right, C = center, L = left, T = top, and B = bottom.)

William Aplin
114LB

John Blaustein
25(all)

John Bryan
102(2nd from T)

Burpee Seed Co.
120(2nd from B)

Walter Chandoha
30, 109(2nd from B), 113T, 125(2nd from B)

Clyde Childress
101T

Derek Fell
97, 98C, 102(two at B), 103B, 104(2nd from B), 112BL, 119C, 123T, 124B, 126T

Pamela Harper
100LC, 101(two at B), 106TR, 107(two at C), 111C, 112BR, 114T, 115B, 116C,B, 120(2nd from T), 123B, 124(two at T), 127T

Michael Landis
115T, 118(2nd from T)

Light Language
12

Fred Lyon
67

George Malave
39

Elvin McDonald
111T

Michael McKinley
52, 100B, 102(2nd from T), 108T, 110B, 114B, 123(2nd from T), 127(2nd from T)

James McNair
14, 18T, 29, 37, 51, 116T, 125T

Jack Napton
105B, 126C

Ortho Photo Library
18B, 26, 33, 34, 35, 38, 41, 53, 100TR, 101(two at T), 104T,B, 105T,C, 106B, 107B, 108C,B, 111B, 112T, LB, 115C, 116C, 119B, 120B, 122T,C, 124(2nd from B), 126B

George Taloumis
109B

Ron Taven
100(2nd from T)

Crafts Stylist
Susan Gilmore

Garden Projects
Michael Landis

Herbal Care Products
Jeanne Rose

Design Associate
Sara Slavin

Special thanks to:
John Benson
Arlene Finger
Susan Fruge
Helen Ganaway
Mary Landis
William and Norma Jean Lathrop
John MacGreggor III
Huntington Gardens
Elvin McDonald
Barbara Rogers
Betty Rollins
Kathy Rossi
Barbara Tracy
Myrtle Wolf
Inga Vesik

Produced under the authorization of The American Horticultural Society by The Franklin Library and Ortho Books.

Copyright © 1978, 1982 by Ortho Books. Special contents © 1982 by The American Horticultural Society. All rights reserved under International and Pan-American Copyright Conventions.

Every effort has been made at the time of publication to guarantee the accuracy of the names and addresses of information sources and suppliers and in the technical data contained. However, the subscriber should check for his own assurance and must be responsible for selection and use of suppliers and supplies, plant materials, and chemical products.

No portion of this book may be reproduced in any form or by any means without permission first being requested and obtained in writing from The American Horticultural Society, c/o The Franklin Library, Franklin Center, Pennsylvania, 19091. Portions of this volume previously appeared in the Ortho Book *The World of Herbs & Spices*.

Library of Congress Catalog Card Number 81-71120

Printed in the United States of America

12 11 10 9 8 7 6 5 4 3 2 1

A Special Message from
The American Horticultural Society

The versatility of herbs and spices makes them favorites of gardeners. The aromatic rosemary, to take just one example, is suitable for a ground cover, for a hedge, for planting in an herb garden with a theme, for making tea, and for seasoning a variety of dishes.

The charm of herbs and spices also lies in their association with particular virtues and customs. In the sixteenth century, Sir Thomas More wrote of his fondness for rosemary, "not only because my bees love it, but because 'tis the herb sacred to remembrance, and therefore to friendship." Shakespeare's mentions of these plants are frequent. It is not our purpose, however, to dwell upon the fascinating lore of herbs and spices or upon the beautiful references to them in literature. This is a book to help beginning and experienced gardeners learn to grow a wide range of herbs and spices, whether indoors or out, and to use these adaptable plants in landscapes, kitchens, and crafts.

Herbs are sturdy and respond well to good basic care. With information on how to plant an herb or spice and what its needs are concerning light, temperature, soil, and moisture, you will be able to use whatever space is available for an herb garden, whether you have only a few glazed pots or acres of land. In addition, methods of propagation, harvesting, and preservation are presented here in a clear fashion.

Whether you cluster your herbs and spices in beds of their own or scatter them around your garden, their colors, forms, fragrances, and growth patterns will be important aspects of any plan. We consider these elements in relation to various garden designs. Would you like a gray and silver herb garden? We'll tell you which plants have the lovely hues appropriate to such a setting. With our help, you can create an herb plot just to attract bees. You will enjoy their humming on a warm, thyme-scented afternoon.

Summer will end, but there are imaginative ways to preserve the aromatic and wholesome properties of your plants. With our directions, you can make a miniature nosegay of dried herbs and spices in the Elizabethan manner or prepare some nutritious rose hip jelly for a friend. There are simple recipes for many herbal pleasures from pesto sauce to moist and dry potpourris. Your herb and spice garden can be a charming introduction to cooking, flower arranging, and other delights of life.

Gilbert S. Daniels
President

CONTENTS

Introduction   10

Throughout recorded history herbs and spices have contributed to the cuisines, medicines, and lore of numerous cultures. Today there is a renewal of interest in their attributes and their use in the home landscape. In this chapter you will learn, briefly, the history of the use of herbs and spices as well as how to define and distinguish between them.

The Basics of Herb Gardening   16

Herbs and spices are quite adaptable but, like common flowers and vegetables, they need good basic care. This chapter outlines what you need to know about light, food, and water for your herb garden. You will also learn methods of potting and propagation. Then, at harvest time, with proper snipping and clipping, you reap your reward.

Herbs and Spices in the Landscape 36

Trim your landscape with herbs and spices or give them, as is the custom, a place of their own. Whether you decide to put your herb garden on a hillside or in a container this chapter will help you plan it. You will find suggestions for designing a Shakespeare, medieval, or tea garden. Make a lovely gray and silver retreat with rosemary, lamb's ears, and other herbs suggested for this purpose.

Culinary Herbs and Spices 54

Your willingness to experiment with unfamiliar ingredients will help you give a lift to old recipes and enlarge your repertoire in the kitchen. Beverages, breads, candies, condiments, salads, sauces: these are a few of the foods considered in this chapter that can be enhanced with herbs and spices. Easy-to-follow recipes are provided.

Creative Uses for Herbs and Spices 78

Many herbs and spices make ideal presents and decorations. Capture the fragrance and beauty of the garden in a potpourri, a garland, or a scented soap. Create natural colors for dyeing or for use in home-grown makeup and other cosmetics. You can learn to make these and other herbal delights by following the simple directions in this chapter.

Plant Selection Guide

Learn the characteristics of many herbs and spices suitable for cultivation in your garden. The information concerning color, size, and cultural needs is clearly presented. The herbs described have varied uses; there are plants for fragrance, for dyeing, and, of course, for flavoring and teas. Common names as well as botanical ones are given.

Commercial Herbs and Spices

This chapter describes the herbs and spices that may be obtained from commercial suppliers. Many of these plants can be cultivated and preserved at home. A handy guide ranges from agrimony to yerba maté, giving botanical names, origins, parts of the plant used, flavors, forms, and uses as well as preferred location (indoors or out).

HERBS AND SPICES

Herbs and spices arrive as an array of
exotic imports or with the harvest of a home
garden. Both fresh or dried and preserved,
they serve countless uses.

INTRODUCTION

Herbs and spices, famous for their sensual and utilitarian qualities, have delighted mankind for thousands of years.

It is possible that herbs and spices were first employed in a systematic way in Mesopotamia and Sumaria three thousand years before the birth of Christ. The first detailed references to various herbs and spices were supplied by the Chinese emperor Shen-Nung, who experimented with them and recorded his conclusions of their properties and effects. The Chinese developed an herbal lore practiced and expanded upon by herbalists prized for their knowledge, as well as feared for the power tinged with shamanism which they commanded. The ancient Chinese custom of perfuming the mouth with cloves before speaking to the emperor required an expert who could provide the aromatic plant at all times of the year. The ability of certain spices to preserve meats demanded an herbalist with a keen knowledge of plants and health.

In Egypt it was recorded that in 1500 B.C. Pharaoh Thothmes III sent an expedition to Syria charged in part to seek new medicinal plants. India was for centuries the center of the herb and spice trade for both the East and the West. Turmeric, cardamom, and cloves have been cultivated in the Indus Valley since 1000 B.C.

The Greeks were the first to begin cataloging plants in about 500 B.C., and herbs and spices were an important part of this flora. In 300 B.C. Theophrastus of Eresus compiled a *History of Plants* which included many plants from the Far East introduced by Alexander the Great's returning armies. The Romans continued the cataloging, notably in Pliny the Elder's *Natural History*. The Romans also recognized the economic importance of trade in herbs and spices with the East and securely monopolized it.

The first comprehensive treatment of medicinal herbs was written about A.D. 50 by a Roman doctor, Pedanius Dioscordis. His *De Materia Medica* was the foundation upon which all subsequent herbals were based.

Although the Goths overran the western Roman Empire in the 5th century, Constantine's eastern empire continued trade with India until Arab conquests cut off European trade routes with the Far East. From the 7th to the 15th centuries the Arab caliphs controlled the spice markets.

During the Middle Ages, some of the myths and deliberately frightening fictions of the ancient herbalists descended again on continental Europe. Nonetheless, herbs and spices continued to be grown and studied, particularly in Benedictine and other monasteries.

With the onset of the Renaissance the search for new trade routes to India was renewed. Columbus was searching for such routes for spices from the Indies on his voyage of discovery. Returning to Spain from the New World he brought quantities of allspice, red pepper, and cocoa. Together with the native European plants and those brought back from the true Indies, these became the basis of the Renaissance gardens. Many kinds of herbs for numerous uses were planted together in elaborate formal patterns. The first printed herbal was published in Rome in 1484, and in the 1500s the Univer-

Top: A medieval herbalist is shown in a 12th-century manuscript illustration.

Above: A miniature of the 15th century shows the gathering of sage.

Opposite: Fields of flowering yellow mustard could be found in Dijon, France, or anywhere in the United States.

sity of Padua had developed an herb garden that successfully maintained plants from the Far East, the New World, and Europe.

European settlers in the Americas brought an array of herbs from their homelands. The English planted mint, thyme, and angelica. The Germans, Scots, and Irish who came to Pennsylvania planted their favorites: dill, savory, and calendulas. Adapting their plants to new climates and soil conditions, the colonists also domesticated such wild native herbs as goldenrod, sassafras, and bayberry.

Defining the Terms

The distinction between an herb and a spice is more subjective than scientific. In fact your determination of the differing qualities of herbs and spices will be entirely subjective, depending on your own likes and dislikes. Cooks, perfumers, chemists, and horticulturists can provide helpful information and distinctions, but in the final analysis no expert can tell you more about the varied natural substances, collectively labeled herbs and spices, than you can discover through your own senses.

Botanically speaking, the word "herb" is derived from the Latin *herba*, which means grass or green crops. Most herbs are herbaceous plants, that is, plants whose stems are soft and succulent rather than woody; such plants die entirely or die down to the root after flowering. In ordinary language, the word herb refers to any of those plants, both herbaceous and woody, whose leaves, flowers, seeds, roots, bark, or other parts are used for flavor, fragrance, medicines, cosmetics, or dyes. Thus, "herb" is a very general and comprehensive category of plant life, including many weeds, grasses, and hardy vegetables, along with flowers, shrubs, and trees.

A question often arises about the pronunciation of the word herb. The old English form was "erbe." It was spelled that way until late in the 15th century when the *h* was added and the final *e* dropped, although the *h* remained silent until the 19th century. Then the *h* began to be pronounced by people who wished to disassociate themselves from the Cockney accent which generally drops the initial *h* in a word. It is still pronounced *h*erb in England, Canada, and New England. Either way is correct.

The word "spice" comes from the Latin *species*, which means ally. Spices may be thought of as the allies or complements of other substances. They are really defined by how we use them and how they stimulate our senses. A spice may be any strongly flavored or aromatic substance, obtained from seeds, roots, fruits, flowers, or bark of a plant that is used in the same ways as herbs.

Often entire plants are regarded as herbs while only the useful parts or derivatives of plants are true spices. The climbing orchid *Vanilla planifolia*, for example, is not itself a spice. Only its long, podlike fruit that is fermented, cured, and marketed as vanilla bean, and the extract prepared by macerating the bean in an alcohol solution, are spices. On the other hand, the entire sprig of parsley, leaves and stem, is the herb parsley. In fact, the stems of many herbs are richer in the essential oils than their leaves.

To complicate the distinction between the terms, two different names for parts of the same plant can be used. For instance, the plant commonly called coriander (*Coriandum sativum*) produces green leaves and stems that when eaten fresh or dried are referred to as the herb cilantro or Chinese parsley. The seeds of the plant, however, fall into the spice category as coriander.

The two terms came into common usage when the early European herbalists referred to useful or delightful plants grown locally as herbs. Those that grew in tropical regions and were transported, for example, by camel along the ancient Cinnamon Route and then via ship, were called spices. The local herbs were ready to use in fresh form, although they were also dried or preserved by other means for later use. But in those days spices were transported only in dry form to reduce their bulk.

Herbs are still considered as temperate-zone plants that may be used fresh or dried and usually in whole leaf form, while spices are categorized as being cultivated in the East and the tropics and are dried whole or cut and powdered. In reality, traditional spices such as ginger root are now grown in temperate climates in home gardens. The real importance of herbs and spices is not what distinguishes them from one another but rather what unites them: the pleasures they give us and their utility in cooking and a variety of other uses.

When you think of spices and herbs as the complements of other substances, you get a notion of proportions. A quart of rice pudding is flavored with a few drops of vanilla or a grating of nutmeg. A single bay leaf in a turkey pie is enough. A few drops of lavender oil will scent a bar of soap. Herbs and spices are used in very small quantities because of the potency of their essential oils; thus, they hold great appeal to both the gardener with limited space and the cook on a limited budget.

You need not always consider an herb or spice merely as a complement to other foods; they may also be featured as a tasty food in themselves. Persian cooks, for example, flavor parsley with lamb; crystallized ginger root is well known in the Orient as a confection; and Italian pesto, made of fresh ground basil leaves, is used with pasta in the same manner as a meat sauce.

The utility of herbs and spices is not limited to our sensual enjoyment of their flavors and aromas. Green herbs are in some cases as rich in nutrients as their vegetable relatives. In the days before the invention of refrigerators, freezers, and safe canning methods, the spices that preserved foods literally maintained life.

European markets offer herb seedlings and the yield of mature harvests.

A Renaissance for Herbs

A walk through an herb garden can be like a botanical world tour. Plants we use as herbs and spices have been gathered from the temperate and tropical zones of both hemispheres. Many of our favorite seasonings and fragrances from the arid Mediterranean region grow alongside natives from North America and tropical islands.

When you survey the spice shelves in a market, you will see exotic products from all corners of the globe. Many flavorings and fragrances we now take for granted were once costly treasures or not available at any price.

Native American herbs and spices were among the first New World treasures. But by the early years of this century, most Americans were unfamiliar with herbs other than the ubiquitous parsley, mint, and a few other basic seasonings. Recently, however, there has been a tremendous escalation in the popularity, production, and distribution of herbs and spices as garden seed, plants, and dried preparations. Nursery personnel report a doubling in the sales of herbs, and retail sales of preserved forms of herbs and spices have also doubled in the past decade. What lies behind this revival of interest in herbs and spices?

At the forefront is the burgeoning interest in well-prepared foods. Americans are considering the preparation of food more creatively and experimenting with the cookery of different cultures. As the demand for international flavorings has increased, so has the variety of seasonings available at the supermarket or from mail-order suppliers. More people are taking cooking lessons, buying cookbooks, and discovering the secrets of great cuisines that employ a variety of herbs and spices. As a result many cooks have also learned to use seasonings to add zestful flavors to simple dishes and impart a bit of excitement to convenience foods.

The health food movement has also called our attention to herbs and spices. No longer does the phrase "health foods" mean simply a diet of yogurt and sprouts. Many ethnic influences, greater supplies of fresh chemical-free produce, and creative uses of seasonings as indispensable ingredients have led to a new cuisine that is receiving growing respect and

Chinese herbalists today offer the same products that they have throughout the centuries.

popularity. Many cooks are thrilled to discover the difference in taste imparted by fresh herbs compared with the dried, store-bought variety.

The popularity of herbs has also grown with the increased interest in gardening. More and more people are discovering the pleasures and economy of homegrown produce. After starting with a few basic herbs, they are soon eager to try others. Nurseries have met the interest by supplying more of the old species as well as new varieties.

A resurgence of interest by many people in traditional crafts has also led to the cultivation and employment of herbs and spices in traditional ways. Such things as dried herb bouquets are not only made at home for fun but highly skilled craftspeople are also using herbs and spices in papers, candles, dyes for natural fibers, and in numerous other almost forgotten arts.

We have rediscovered the simple, sensual pleasure of potpourris and other scents reminiscent of the Victorian garden. Incenses entered the mainstream of our culture in the 1960s. Now many people are harvesting or purchasing herbs and spices to create fragrances and natural cosmetics. Additionally, many herbs and spices flourish in a wide range of climates, are adaptable to either garden or container plantings, require little maintenance, and use water sparingly.

Two herb gardeners spend many
pleasurable hours each week in their garden.
As they discover new plants to grow, the
garden expands over a steep hillside by
means of terraces and raised beds.

THE BASICS OF HERB GARDENING

If you know the fundamentals of how to grow, harvest, and preserve herbs, the bounty of your herb garden can be generous and very satisfying.

In spite of all the lore surrounding the use of herbs and spices, growing them is no more difficult than growing ordinary flowers and vegetables. In this book the *ideal* conditions for *optimum* growth are given, but remember that most hardy plants can be grown under conditions that are less than ideal and still maintain satisfactory growth and yield.

As with other garden plants, herbs and spices can be classed as either annuals, biennials, or perennials. *Annuals* complete their life cycle in one growing season and new plants must be set out or propagated from seed each year. *Biennials* complete their life cycle in two growing seasons, while *perennials* live for many years though a portion of the plant may die back at the end of each growing season. Generally you will be successful with annual herbs by planting and growing them right along with your other annual vegetables and flowers. Treat the perennial plants just as you would ornamentals and you will probably be pleased with their response.

It would be nearly impossible to satisfy the ideal conditions for all herbs in the small garden space usually devoted to them, but you can count on plenty of seasonings if you consider herbs as a group and think of them as an extension of the vegetable garden. With many herbs such as mint, lemon balm, and tarragon, the problem is keeping them under control once they are established in the garden.

Many herbs are hardy, easy to grow, practically immune to diseases and pests, adaptable to many types of soil and growing conditions, and quite tolerant of drought and neglect. Of course, like any group of plants, they will reward you well if you pay attention to their basic needs.

The Outdoor Garden

Whether you have a few plants growing near the kitchen door, rows of herbs among vegetables or cutting flowers, or a large formal garden, the techniques of outdoor gardening remain the same in most climates.

Selecting the best exposure. Most herbs and spices require full sunlight for at least 5 to 8 hours a day. Quite a few are tolerant of partial shade and some forest natives enjoy full shade. A list of plants suitable for planting in partial or full shade may be found on page 52 or check the individual plant requirements in the Plant Selection Guide on pages 96–127.

Preparing the site and soil. Most plants recommended for home gardens in this book prefer well-drained soil. Exceptions to the rule include horseradish, ginger, sweet flag, and woodruff, which all enjoy moist rich soil around their roots. A few plants even grow directly in water. (Listings of bog and water plants may be found on page 52.) For the vast majority of herbs and spices an ideal planting site would be a gentle incline with sandy soil.

If your garden does not have good natural drainage you have two options: a raised bed or a soil amendment.

Right: Garden centers around the world offer herb transplants to give the gardener a head start on the growing season.

Below: Raised beds serve well as planting areas for herbs, since with the proper planting mix you can be assured of the good drainage most herbs need.

Raised beds. Raised beds have been used in herb gardening since ancient times. All you need is something that will hold about 6 inches of soil above the natural ground level. Railroad ties, fence posts, cement blocks, or stones can be used as the bed walls, or you can use redwood boards held in place with 2 by 4s. A wood header board nailed to the top will let you sit while you maintain and harvest the herbs or just enjoy their textures and fragrances.

Once you have built the bed, fill it with fresh soil. If it is a small bed, you can purchase one of the packaged synthetic soils such as Jiffy-Mix or Redi-Earth formulated to provide good drainage and balanced support for the roots.

For larger beds it is economical and easy to make your own mix.

Planting mix

9 cubic feet fine sand	5 pounds 5–10–10 fertilizer
9 cubic feet peat moss	7 pounds ground limestone
9 cubic feet ground bark	1 pound iron sulphate

Mix these ingredients well and fill the bed. These amounts will give you 6 inches of soil in a bed measuring about 6 feet by 6 feet.

Soil amendment. If you do not want a raised bed for your herbs, you can improve drainage and soil by amending your soil. Excavate the planting area to a depth of about 1 foot, keeping the topsoil and the subsoil in two separate piles. Break up any large clods. Spread 2 to 4 inches of crushed rock or large gravel in the bottom of the hole.

Add 1 part sand to 3 parts subsoil, mix well, and fill the area a little over halfway. Then blend in 1 part organic matter (compost, manure, peat moss, leaf mold, or sawdust) to 3 parts topsoil and fill the planting area.

Use a soil-test kit to determine the pH of your soil if you are in doubt or have a sample checked at your nearby agricultural extension service office. The pH is a measure of relative acidity. If the pH is 7 the soil is neutral, below 7 the soil is acidic and above 7 it is alkaline. Most herbs enjoy a pH in the range of 6.0 to 7.5, but a few prefer more alkaline soil. If your soil is found to be too acidic, add 5 pounds finely ground limestone to each 100 square feet of planting area in order to raise the pH about a half to a full point. Alkaline soil can be changed the same amount by adding ½ pound ground sulphur or 3 pounds aluminum sulfate or iron sulfate to each 100 square feet.

Planting the garden. Seed and transplants of common herbs are available at garden centers, nurseries, plant shops, or from mail-order suppliers. You will have to order the more unusual varieties from specialized catalogues (see page 142) or secure them from herb-growing friends.

If you want only a few plants of each variety, it's easiest to buy seedlings from a local source. They can be easily transplanted and establish themselves quickly.

To transplant a plant from a small container into the ground, follow these simple steps: The day before the move, water the plant thoroughly so that the root system and soil will hold together well.

Make a hole in the garden soil large enough to accommodate the rootball.

Hold the pot with one hand and put the other hand over the top, with the plant stem between two fingers.

Turn the pot upside down and with a downward motion tap the rim against the edge of a table or bench to loosen the rootball. Then lift the pot away.

Slip the plant into the hole you have prepared and align the level of the soil around the rootball with ground level. Add a little more soil around the plant and firm with your fingers to eliminate any air pockets. Water thoroughly and put identification labels at the base of the plant.

If you want a head start on the season, you can begin seeds indoors in late winter (see page 24). Most seeds thrive better, however, if sown directly in the garden as soon as all danger of frost is past and the soil has begun to warm up. Some seeds that require a long germination period can be planted in the late fall for the following growing season. Follow the planting times recommended on the seed packets for your local climate.

Many herbs look best and grow well when planted in large expanses or clumps rather than neat rows. Rake the freshly prepared bed and scatter the seeds evenly over the area. Cover with soil to the depth recommended on the seed packet—usually twice the seed diameter. Firm the topsoil with your hands or a board and water the planting area with a fine spray.

If you want to plant seeds in rows, make shallow furrows in the prepared soil with a rake. Sow the seeds in the furrows following the recommended distance between seeds given on the packet. Firm and moisten as described above.

Always label all seed beds as soon as you have planted them so you will know what is growing in each location.

If you share your garden with hungry birds, cover the planting area with screening until the seeds germinate. Keep the soil moist, but never soggy, throughout germination. Normally, annuals take about 2 weeks and perennials about 3 to 4 weeks or longer to germinate; check the seed packet.

You can lengthen the harvest of herbs with a short growing season, such as coriander and borage, by making successive sowings several weeks apart.

When the seedlings are up and have formed two pairs of true leaves, thin out overcrowded areas. The thinnings of culinary herbs are delicately flavored and can be used in foods, or you can transplant healthy seedlings to another spot in the garden or to containers.

When the plants are several inches tall, they may benefit from a covering of mulch. Mulches keep weeds under control, retain moisture, set off the plants visually, and keep the soil at a cool and even temperature. Organic materials such as bark chips, chunky peat moss, pine needles, and straw, or small gravels, are logical companions to herbs. Plastic sheeting is not advisable around herbs because it tends to retain too much surface moisture and does not allow enough air circulation.

Watering and feeding. Frequent light spraying with a garden hose is a poor method of watering because it supplies moisture only to the surface of the soil. Herbs need deep soaking that penetrates the ground at least 12 inches. Use a handheld hose if you have the patience, but a soaker hose is more

To transplant herbs into the garden, prepare a hole in amended soil.

Tap the plant from its container and position it in the ground, matching the soil level of the transplant with that of the ground.

Firm the soil (above); then water the plant and add a label (below).

convenient and effective. Let it run for a couple of hours each time you water, preferably in the morning so that the plants will have plenty of water during the hot part of the day.

Avoid overwatering, but at the same time never allow the soil to dry out completely. For routine watering some gardeners use a rule of thumb— don't water until you see a few leaves beginning to wilt, then water thoroughly. A more accurate test is to insert your finger into the soil which, if it is beginning to dry out a half-inch below the surface, needs water.

A few herbs and spices require moist soil at all times and some prefer it very dry. Consult the specific requirements on pages 96–127.

Although herbs do not need the large amounts of fertilizer that many other plants do, they respond to moderate feedings once or twice a year. Feed in the spring with a balanced fertilizer such as 5–10–5 and again in late summer to help carry the herbs on through fall. Too much fertilizer makes the soil overly rich and results in lush foliage that has only small amounts of fragrant oils. However, some of the plants mentioned in this book—such as the flowering shrubs—require more and heavier feedings than the normal herbs for optimum growth.

Controlling pests and diseases. The fragrant oils in herb leaves that make them attractive to people also repel certain insects and make the plants resistant to disease. Occasionally pests such as aphids or red spider mites will attack herbs. Hose them off edible herbs with a strong stream of water. Herbs not intended for culinary or cosmetic use can be treated with a chemical spray to control insects.

Keep an eye out for pests on roses and other flowering shrubs that grow alongside herbs. Spray with appropriate chemicals at the first sign of attack, unless you plan to eat the herbs, in which case remove the infestation with a strong jet of water or cut away the infested parts. Always spray chemicals carefully to avoid wind drift onto edible herbs.

Slugs and snails agree with cooks about the taste of tender young herbs. Should they move in on your garden, immediately sprinkle the area with snail bait, following the directions on the label. For use around culinary herbs, select formulas recommended for vegetables. If these pests are common in your garden, put out the bait when you first plant to protect the seedlings.

Protecting herbs in winter. After the leaves of perennial plants wither in the fall, cut the stalks down to ground level. In cold regions tender evergreen perennials should be dug up, potted in containers, and moved indoors before frost.

New Englander Barbara Rogers advises, "With a little extra attention to the less hardy varieties, the herb gardener in the north can be just as successful as one in a kinder climate. The annuals are fast growing enough to mature in a short season and most perennial herbs are winter hardy.

"Rosemary, bay, lemon verbena, sweet marjoram, and some of the thymes are not hardy and can be brought indoors to winter over and all make attractive houseplants in the process. Lemon verbena will wilt, lose its leaves, and appear to be dying. This is just its natural seasonal defoliation. Give it light, but water sparingly and, as spring approaches, it will sprout new leaves."

Some people like to extend the season for fresh herbs by digging annuals that are still productive from the outdoor garden and potting them for growing indoors. When you move herbs indoors, wash them in soapy water to get rid of any aphids or red spiders that may be hiding and which could spread to other houseplants. Be sure to rinse the plants well after washing them.

In regions where the ground freezes, mulch the outdoor perennial herb garden after the first freeze. Plants should remain frozen all winter and not alternately freeze and thaw. Cover thickly with straw, leaves, marsh or salt hay, or evergreen boughs to allow air to get through. Leave the mulch on until all frost danger is past.

Confining the spread of herbs. If you want just a small area of tarragon, mint, or other herb that spreads rapidly, plant it in a clay pot with the soil about an inch below the rim, then sink the pot into the ground deep enough that the soil levels in the pot and the ground are even. Instead of pots you can sink a wooden box, header boards, or metal strips 6 to 8 inches into the soil.

The Container Garden Indoors and Outdoors

Herbs and spices are good candidates for container gardening. They are easy to grow, adaptable, and enjoy the good drainage that pots and other containers allow. Often herbs look more attractive thus displayed than tucked away among other plants outdoors. Best of all, potted herbs allow for versatility in meeting their cultural needs throughout the year. The containers can be shifted around the garden, deck, patio, or from room to room as sun patterns change with the seasons. For gardeners with limited space, growing herbs in containers is an obvious convenience.

Before potting, add vermiculite to container soil to facilitate good drainage.

In a sunny window, under artificial lighting, or with a combination of the two, herbs can keep on growing all winter. Then they can be transferred outdoors when the weather warms up or, if their simple growing requirements can be met, remain indoors year around.

The potting soil. The easiest and surest choice is packaged potting mix. It provides good drainage and can be used without further amendment for most plants described in this book. If a particular herb requires rich soil (see pages 96–127) just add an equal quantity of organic matter such as leaf mold or peat moss to the packaged mix. If very fast drainage is required, mix an equal part of perlite or sand with the packaged formula.

Many plants can be grown indoors using hydroponic gardening which requires no soil whatsoever. This subject is too complex to explore in this book, but many herbs, such as mint or parsley, can be adapted to this specialized form of gardening in water with regular additions of nutrients. Most garden centers offer hydroponic units and supplies.

Hold the pot securely and tap the rootball out of the container.

Potting and transplanting. You may either plant one kind of herb per pot or combine several in a container garden. A variety of plants in one container should share similar requirements for soil, water, and light.

Make sure the container is clean and cover the drainage hole with a piece of broken pottery, concave side down, or a piece of galvanized screen to keep soil from washing into and clogging the drainage hole. Put a little potting soil in the bottom.

Remove the plant from its old container, as described on page 19, and place the plant in the new container with enough soil in the bottom so that the plant sits comfortably with the top of its rootball about an inch below the rim. Add soil mix around the sides and with your fingers compress the soil all around the roots to eliminate air pockets. Water until the container drains.

Position the plant in the pot and firm the soil (above). Water well (below).

It is a good idea to remove plants from their containers about once a year to see if the rootball has become potbound. If you have noticed that leaves wilt in spite of good cultural habits, it is probably time to repot the plant.

If you discover the roots are overgrown, loosen them by hand, shake off the loose soil, and repot in a container that is one size larger. An alternative method is to cut through the root system from top to bottom in two places, then across the bottom, and remove about a third of the rootball. Prune away the same amount of foliage growth and repot in a container that is one size larger.

Planting a mossed herb basket. Don't overlook a moss-lined basket as a

Top, left to right: Make a collar of moss around the basket top; line the inside and bottom; trim away straggly moss.

Bottom, left to right: Add about 2 inches of moist soil; plant through holes in moss sides, adding soil at each new planting level, and plant top; water the newly planted basket.

container for your herbs. There is something about the look of a mossy hanging basket near the kitchen door or wherever there is good sunlight that seems just right for a mixture of culinary herbs. It's easy to make and rewards you with seasonings for many months.

Materials needed:

Wire basket, available in many sizes and shapes from garden centers, to hang from the ceiling or flat against a wall

Hardware for hanging

Green sphagnum moss to line basket

Soil mix

Seedlings (about 2 dozen for a 10-inch basket)

Soak the moss in a container of water for about 15 minutes while you attach the hardware to hang the basket.

Take a piece of moss about 6 inches square and squeeze the water from it. Fold it in half with the leafy side out and slide in between the top two horizontal wires of the basket by pressing the moss together. When you let go, the natural springiness of the moss will hold it in place.

Push the piece of moss against a vertical wire and align with the top of the basket. Insert another piece of moss in the same way and move it tightly against the first piece. Repeat this procedure until there is a tight collar of moss around the top of the basket.

With large pieces of moss line the inside and bottom of the basket, overlapping each piece so that soil cannot leak through. After lining, trim any straggly pieces with scissors.

Put about 2 inches of moist soil in the bottom. Poke a hole from the side through the moss so that a plant's rootball can be inserted. Bend the wires if necessary to enlarge the opening. Remove the seedling from its container and gently shake off loose soil. Insert the roots through the wire frame and moss so that the rootball lies on the surface of the soil mix and the crown of the plant (where the stem and the root merge) just touches the inside of the moss lining. Place more plants in this way until the bottom row is complete.

When the bottom of the basket has been planted, add another inch or so of soil and insert another row of plants around the basket, staggering the placement of the plants to allow good circulation of air and sufficient sunlight. Continue planting until you reach the moss collar. Then add soil to within one inch of the basket top. Plant the top as you would any other container.

As the plants grow you can train them as you wish by positioning the stems with pins or bent pieces of wire stuck into the mossed basket. Feed and water them as you would ordinary container plants and harvest them frequently to encourage full growth.

The right light. Although most herbs enjoy full sun, containerized plants lack the insulation around their roots that a garden provides. Potted plants outdoors should be in partial shade during the hottest part of a summer day, or positioned so that at least the roots are in the shade.

Check the recommended light for each plant indoors or out and find a spot with that amount of light. During the year as the sun shifts its position throughout the day, you will be able to reposition the pot. That is part of the advantage of container gardening.

The indoor gardener might consider a window greenhouse, especially for culinary herbs. Easy-to-install prefabricated units are available or you can build your own with a simple framework of 2 by 4s encased in heavy plastic sheets.

Artificial lighting. If you do not have a place indoors that gets at least 5 hours of direct sun a day, add artificial lighting. Artificial light can also be the sole source of light, in which case you have to assure that the plants get the full spectrum of light they need. It can come from various combinations of fluorescent and incandescent lights or, more easily, from the wide-spectrum fluorescent lights. These tubes—available in standard fixture lengths—come close to providing all the wavelengths in natural daylight in the proper proportions for plants to thrive.

Fixtures can be mounted underneath shelves, window sills, or kitchen cupboards to shine down on counter tops, or hidden inside cabinets. With hood reflectors to bounce light down on the leaves, units can be attached to carts, hung from the ceiling, or supported over tabletops.

Herbs can flourish all year long in a closet, basement, or hallway. The designing gardener can install herb and spice light gardens that are as attractive as any outdoor bed or window display. Lights should operate 14 to 18 hours per day. Install a simple automatic timer that will turn the lamps on and off regardless of your memory or schedule.

The top of the foliage should never be closer than 5 or 6 inches from the lamp and never farther away than 15 to 18 inches. Most prefabricated light units have adjustable mountings to raise the light as plants grow. With immovable fixtures, set small plants on inverted pots or saucers so that you can take away the supports as the plants grow taller. When gardening with

For inspired cooking, grow a few culinary herbs in a window greenhouse off the kitchen.

An herb garden can be grown indoors in any location with the use of artificial light in a plant stand with reflecting hood.

artificial light, no special plant care is needed beyond the general maintenance guidelines given in this book.

Water and food. It is time to water your plant if the soil a half-inch below the surface is dry. Overwatering is the biggest hazard to plants indoors; too often they are drowned with kindness. Putting your finger a half-inch into the soil is the most reliable way to tell when it is time to water. Apply water until it runs through to the saucer. Let it stand for half an hour, then pour off any excess water from the drainage saucer.

Do not allow the soil to dry out completely between waterings or the rootball will shrink and then water will just run down the inside of the pot and escape rather than soaking into the soil. If a plant has gone so long without water that the soil is hard and dry, submerge the pot in water and let it soak for several minutes or until air bubbles stop rising from the soil surface. Then let it drain as you would for a normal watering.

The moisture of the soil in outdoor containers should be checked every couple of days. Plants in containers usually require watering more often than those growing in the garden.

Container-grown plants do not have as many natural nutrients available to them as do their garden relatives, so they benefit from regular additions of one of the balanced houseplant fertilizers. Always water the plant before feeding. Fertilize mildly from early spring to fall when the plants are in active growth, but use only about half the strength and apply only half as often as recommended on the product label.

The right atmosphere. Indoor herbs appreciate extra humidity. Pebbles in the drainage tray with a little water in the bottom will increase the humidity of the air immediately around the plants. A dish of water set among the plants helps in a similar way. Misting the foliage as you do other houseplants not only adds humidity but helps keep the leaves clean. It is a good idea to immerse the foliage in tepid water every few weeks to wash away any accumulated dust or household grease.

Average house temperatures are generally conducive to growing most herbs and spices. They appreciate lower temperatures at night, but never down to freezing. Likewise, they cannot tolerate extended periods of excessive heat. Always keep plants away from drafts of air conditioners or heating systems and far away from any gas appliance. Keep them near a window that can be opened, provided the temperature is above freezing. Turn the containers a quarter-round every time you water to insure even growth from exposure to light and air.

Pest control. As with plants grown outdoors, in the event that pests attack indoor herbs being used for cooking or cosmetics, the plants should be washed *only* with a strong spray from a garden hose or immersed and washed in a mild solution of soap and water—not detergent—and thoroughly rinsed. Herbs that are not to be eaten or used on the skin can be sprayed with malathion. Be sure to spray both sides of the leaves.

Herb and Spice Propagation

In addition to direct seeding in the outdoor garden as outlined on page 19, there are several methods of starting new plants. Most herbs and spices are prolific and will reseed or produce new shoots for new plants if allowed.

Starting seeds indoors. To obtain a head start on spring, you can sow seed indoors several weeks before it would be possible outdoors. Then, when planting time arrives, you have transplants ready for the garden or containers. This is a particular advantage if your growing season is short or when starting perennials that take a long time to germinate. It is not advisable, however, to start anise, borage, caraway, and other such plants with long taproots indoors, unless you start them in separate large containers. Even then, they do not transplant easily, and it is safer to wait until the danger of frost is past and to seed them directly in the garden.

Check individual plant recommendations on pages 96–127 to see which grow easily from seed. Sow seeds in late winter in nursery flats, trays, or any clean shallow container that has good drainage.

Fill the container to within ½ inch of the top with thoroughly dampened vermiculite. (Some gardeners sow the seed directly into a well-draining soil mix.) Mark off rows 2 inches apart and set seeds to the depth and spacing recommended on the seed packet. Cover the seeds by spreading the surface soil with your hand and pressing down gently. Mist lightly and label the planting. Cover the container with glass or a layer of plastic, or enclose it in a large plastic bag. Keep at 75°F (24°C) and apply no more water until the first green shoots show through the top of the mix. Open the covering every day for about an hour to let in fresh air.

Take off the plastic cover after germination and move the emerging plants to a place with indirect light (no direct sun) and temperatures between 60° and 70°F (16° and 21°C).

When the first true leaves have formed on the seedlings, dig them carefully from the germinating medium and plant them in small containers filled with equal parts of peat moss and vermiculite or any other fast-draining soil mix. With a pencil, make a small hole in the new container soil and set in the seedling so its leaves are ½ inch above the surface. Press firmly around the roots and stem, and water lightly. Several seedlings can be planted in one pot about 1½ inches apart. Don't forget the labels.

Begin giving the plants as much direct sunlight as possible, about 12 hours a day, or use a fluorescent light for 16 hours a day, placed about 6 inches over the seedlings. Adjust the light distance as necessary during the growth of the plants. Water the soil carefully to keep it just moist. In a few weeks the plants will need to be transplanted into larger containers where they can remain or be transplanted later into the garden.

An alternative method is to sow seeds two at a time directly into small blocks made of a growing medium available at most nurseries or garden shops. Simply insert the seeds, water thoroughly, place in a plastic bag on a tray and keep at warm room temperature. Remove the bag after seedlings appear. When it is time to plant in the garden, the growing blocks can be planted directly in the ground.

Start herb and spice plants indoors in flats covered with plastic. Transplant the seedlings after the first true leaves have formed.

Far left: Peat planters of various shapes and sizes make seed starting easy.

Left: Soak the planters in a shallow tray of water; then place two seeds in each one.

A portable A-frame with a plastic covering is useful as an early spring row cover.

When you transfer seedlings grown indoors to the garden, give them some kind of protective plastic cover during their early stages to shelter them from winds, unexpected frost, and birds. The cover must have ventilation to keep the plants from overheating during the day.

At the end of the gardening season collect seed from annuals for growing a new batch of plants again in late winter. Store the seed in an airtight container in a cool dark place or the refrigerator.

Many of the annuals and biennials will seed themselves if you let a few of the plants produce mature seeds. If you live in a cold climate, learn to recognize the emerging seedlings and provide protection to get them started, or take them up and transplant them into containers in a protected environment.

Multiply by dividing. Many indoor and outdoor perennials are best propagated by dividing the plants. Those that grow in clumps, such as tarragon, chives, and sweet woodruff, *need* to be divided every couple of years. Some gardeners divide plants annually; it all depends on how much the plants grow. You may choose to do this chore in the fall after plants go dormant or in the early spring before there is much new growth.

Dividing is simple: Just moisten the ground all around and dig the plant up or take it out of its pot. Pull or cut the root clump into sections and replant each section, with its foliage, into the ground or in containers. Keep the soil moist until the plants become reestablished. If you have an older plant, discard the oldest, compacted center part of the root clump.

Root cuttings. Thyme, tarragon, lemon balm, sage, rosemary, and other plants that send new stems up from their roots can be propagated from root cuttings. Dig pieces of ½-inch diameter roots. Discard the end pieces and cut the remainder into sections about 2 inches long.

Place the pieces of root on top of a flat filled to within an inch of the rim with moist builder's sand or other light growing medium. Cover the root sections with ½ inch of growing medium and water well.

In warm regions encase the flat in clear plastic and set outdoors in the shade. When there is evidence of new growth, remove the protective covering. Set plants out in the garden or in pots when they are several inches high.

In cool climates take the root cuttings in the fall and store them in a cold frame or in a cool (but not freezing) sheltered place until growth appears in the spring. Then transplant them to the garden or individual containers.

Stem cuttings. A generation ago they were called "slips," today we call them stem cuttings. In either case, rooting stem cuttings from perennials is one of the easiest methods of plant propagation, often faster than germination from seed. Check pages 96–127 for those that can be propagated this way.

Anytime during the active growing season take cuttings of 4 to 6 inches from healthy foliage growth near the plant tips. To select a good stem, try bending it sharply. The ones that snap off will root best. Cut the 4- to 6-inch length from the tip of a shoot with a sharp knife or razor blade; make a fresh cut on stems you snap off. Keep the cuttings between layers of dampened paper towel to prevent them from wilting before you can get them into the rooting medium.

Prepare any sort of container that has adequate drainage by filling it with a moistened soilless medium (vermiculite, sand, prepackaged mix, or a combination of these). Strip all foliage from the lower half of the cutting. To further insure success, dip the cut end in rooting hormone powder to stimulate growth. Poke a hole in the moist medium with a pencil and insert the cutting. Firm it in place. Water well.

Encase the entire cutting and container in a plastic bag or cover the top of the container with a clear plastic drinking cup to build up humidity. Set it in

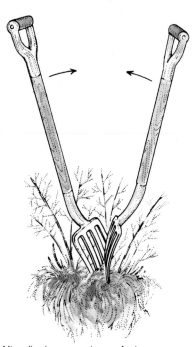

After digging up a clump of a large overgrown perennial, you may find it necessary to use two spading forks, back to back, to divide the plant.

To propagate stem cuttings, first snip 4 to 6 inches of a healthy growing end from a mature plant.

Dip dampened stem into a rooting hormone powder (optional).

After stripping the leaves from the bottom half of the cutting, place it in the growing medium and firm the soil around the plant.

Cover the entire plant with plastic for added humidity. Remove the cover for a few minutes each day to provide fresh air.

a warm place where there is bright indirect light (no direct sun). Remove the cover for a few minutes or so each day to allow fresh air in. When you replace the cover, rotate the container to insure equal exposure to light on all sides of the cutting.

Rooting may take from 1 week for tender-stem herbs to several months for woody-stem ones. When the foliage seems to perk up, remove the plastic covering and put the plant in a good growing area.

When the container seems to be filled with roots, transplant to a larger pot or a well-protected spot in the garden. Keep soil moist until the cutting shows vigorous new growth.

Suckers, which are robust shoots originating in the roots or base of the plants, are usually excellent candidates for rooting by the method just described.

Layering. Propagating perennials by layering is simply giving a natural process a bit of assistance. Many plants layer themselves naturally from branches that come in contact with the soil.

Simply bend a stem so that it will touch the earth just below a leaf node and about 10 inches from the growing tip. With a sharp knife scrape the bottom of slender stems; cut thicker stems about halfway through. Insert a toothpick, matchstick, or a prong of a plastic fork into the cut to wedge it open. Dust either the scraped stem or the wedged cut with rooting hormone powder.

Dig a shallow trench directly underneath the branch and mix the soil you have removed with equal parts peat moss and coarse builder's sand. Bend the prepared branch down into the trench and cover with the soil mix, leaving 6 inches of the stem tip exposed. Pin it in place with a bent wire loop

Layering

Use the toothpick to keep the notch open.

Fill the trench around the notched stem with soil mix, weigh it down with a stone, and water thoroughly.

After new roots around the notch have developed and are well established, cut the stem from the parent plant and transplant the offspring.

or hold it down with a heavy stone. Stake the stem tip upright and slowly soak the soil with water.

In about 6 to 8 weeks carefully remove the soil and check to see if any new roots have formed. When the new roots seem well established, cut the stem from the parent just below the new rootball. Transplant the new plant to a container or directly into the garden.

In cold regions, begin the layering early in the spring so the plant will be ready for transplanting in time to establish itself before frost. If this is not possible and you must do layering in the fall, cover the buried portion with a generous amount of mulch, leaving only the tip exposed.

Harvesting Herbs and Spices

For most herb and spice gardeners, the greatest fun comes at harvest time. Snip bits of French tarragon and parsley to add to a simmering dish. Cut a bouquet of yellow tansy flowers to dry for a centerpiece. Pinch leaves of rose geranium to add to a sweet sachet or float in finger bowls for a special dinner. Clip a cup of chamomile flowers to brew afternoon tea. Catch the seed from a sesame flower just before it bursts open. Or gather big bunches of sweet marjoram just before it blooms.

Harvesting through the season. Most culinary herbs can be used from the time you start thinning the seedlings. The flavor is already there. Snip and clip leaves and sprigs as you need them throughout the growing season. Use scissors, a sharp knife, or your fingernails to take sprigs from a few inches down the stem, just above a set of leaves. Be sure not to take too much growth at once while the plants are young and developing or you may weaken them. Select healthy leaves and pluck out yellow or dead ones at the same time to keep the plants continuously groomed.

As you snip and clip you are also determining the shape of the growing plant, so harvest judiciously. You benefit from enjoying the fresh herbs, and the plants respond with growth that is more lush and full. Leaves that are to be eaten fresh as salad greens—rocket, sorrel, borage, burnet, nasturtium—should be gathered when quite young and tender. Old leaves get too tough to eat. Herbs that send up grassy leaves or stalks directly from the ground—such as chives and parsley—should be cut just above ground level. If you cut off just the tops, you will ruin the plant's appearance and growth habit, and the mature growth will get too tough to eat.

As you harvest throughout the season, pinch out flower buds of tender perennials to increase edible-leaf production. If allowed to flower early, these herbs will grow tough as the seeds set. If you want flowers or seed heads on some plants, let some stems develop through their full cycle. You will probably want to let one or two plants go to seed so they will self-seed the garden or give you seed to harvest and store for planting next season.

Harvesting for preservation. Though you have taken bits and pieces of fresh herbs to use all during the growing season, the special harvest is for preserving. With most herbs it comes just when the flowers are about to open and the oils in the foliage are most heavily concentrated.

Of course, there are exceptions: Sage should be cut when the buds appear and you should wait until the blooms are full to gather hyssop, oregano, and thyme. Cut parsley, borage, salad burnet, and winter savory when the leaves are young.

Harvest early in the morning after the dew has dried but before the hot sun brings out the oils. Some annuals harvested in early summer may grow enough for a second major harvest if your first harvest is not too severe. In the first harvest, cut the plants back to several inches above the ground. For fall-harvest annuals, cut the plants all the way to the ground.

Lavender, marjoram, rosemary, and other shrubby perennials should be cut back to about half the length of the year's growth. Harvest flowers to be

dried for fragrances when they have just opened up and are fresh looking.

Seed heads are ready when they turn color before they open and scatter their seed on the ground. Harvest heads on a warm, dry day by cutting off entire heads or stems and dropping them into paper bags.

Bring all cut herbs indoors out of the sun as soon as possible after harvesting. Keep the different kinds separate and rinse quickly in cool water to remove dirt. Shake off excess water, drain well, then spread on a flat surface. Pick over and discard bad leaves or petals, and label each bunch. If the garden is cooperative and everything does not mature at once, harvest and prepare only one or two bunches of herbs a day.

Roots, tubers, and rhizomes should be harvested in the fall or early spring when they are full of stored plant nutrients. If harvested at other times, the roots will shrink greatly when dried. Remember to save a portion for propagation if you wish.

Preserving the Herbs

Drying is the time-honored method of preserving most leaves, seeds, and flowers. There are different methods of drying, depending on the plant and the desired use. A few herbs can be preserved in salt or vinegar, and quite a few take well to freezing. Select the methods that seem best for you and them. The accompanying chart gives a sampling of commonly used herbs and how they may be preserved.

Herbs to be used in cooking should be dried as whole as possible to retain their flavors. They can then be pulverized between your fingers or in a mortar and pestle when you are ready to use them.

Hang drying. This old method is still the most colorful way of drying the harvest. Take a bunch of one kind of herb, tie the ends of the stems together with string, and hang the bunches upside down in a place that is warm, dry, and away from direct sunlight. Hang them free where air can circulate all around them to prevent mildew. If the room is dusty, place the bunch in a paper bag that has been perforated all around for air circulation. Tie the bag

A well-planned herb garden will include an array of herbs that can be snipped throughout the growing season. It is also important to learn when to harvest each herb for drying.

Methods of Preserving Some Common Herbs

Herb	Freezing	Quick drying	Hang drying	Drying tray	Salt curing
Anise	•	•	•	•	
Basil	•	•	•	•	•
Bay		•		•	
Borage	•		•	•	
Burnet	•	•			•
Caraway			•	•	
Chervil	•	•		•	
Chives	•	•		•	•
Coriander	•	•		•	
Dill		•		•	•
Fennel	•	•			•
Ginger	•				
Marjoram		•	•	•	
Mints	•	•	•		
Oregano	•	•	•	•	
Parsley	•	•	•	•	•
Rosemary	•	•	•	•	
Safflower		•		•	
Saffron		•		•	
Sage	•	•	•	•	
Savory	•	•	•	•	
Sesame		•			
Sorrel		•	•		
Tarragon	•	•	•	•	
Thyme	•	•	•	•	
Woodruff		•	•		

Hang dry herbs upside down in a warm, dry place with good air circulation—and out of direct sunlight.

around the stems. This is a good method for drying seed heads: as the seeds fall they are caught in the bottom of the bag.

Depending on the weather, herbs usually take about 2 weeks to hang dry. They should be crisp and crackly to the touch. Store in labeled jars or bags.

Tray drying. For small quantities of herbs or short pieces of stems and seed heads, drying trays are handy. A simple tray constructed of 1- by 1-inch lumber with screen mesh or cheesecloth stapled to the bottom works fine. Make the trays small enough to hold just a few leaves: 10 by 10 inches is a good size. Put a 1-inch block at each corner if you want to stack several boxes and still get good air circulation. Assembled drying trays are also commercially available.

Let the leaves stay on the stems or strip them off. Make only one layer in each tray. Stir the contents gently every few days to assure even drying. Most herbs dry crisp within a week or 10 days according to the weather. Remove from the trays when crisp.

Dry seed heads the same way, then gently rub the capsules through your hands. A fan on low speed or a natural breeze will blow away the chaff as you drop seed into a tray or bowl.

Quick drying. If you want to dry herbs in a hurry, spread the leaves on a cheesecloth-covered rack in the oven at its lowest temperature. Leave the oven door open and stir the leaves until they are crisp. They should be ready in a few minutes.

Drying roots. Roots, tubers, and rhizomes that are dried before using or for preservation—such as orris, horseradish, or madder—take a bit more time and care because they are so fleshy. Wash the roots thoroughly to remove all dirt, scraping with a knife if necessary, and trim all rootlets from the fleshy part. Slice all large roots. Spread in a thin layer on a wire screen in the sun. Turn the roots two or three times a week to insure that they dry evenly. Bring the roots indoors at night to prevent them from absorbing the night dew.

When the roots have partially dried in the sun, the process may be accelerated by combining several screens and placing the roots in an oven at its lowest temperature setting with the door open. Continue to turn and mix the roots for even drying.

The roots will be thoroughly dried when a slice will snap sharply when bent. Store in containers with tight-fitting lids.

Decorative drying

Drying mediums. To retain the color in resultant flowers or foliage that you plan to use for decorative purposes, try drying in a desiccant. The colorful and paper-crisp dried material can be made into winter bouquets.

You have a choice of several desiccants: household borax powder, fine-grained builder's sand, equal parts cornmeal and borax, or—for truer colors—ground or crushed silica gel crystals.

Prepare the freshly picked flowers for drying by cutting off the stems and replacing them with lengths of florist's wire pushed through the center of the heads. Wrap the wire around leaf clusters.

Start with a wide-mouthed container that has a tight-fitting lid and pour in about 3 inches of the drying medium. Place the flower or herb sprig upright on top, bending the wire flat against the desiccant. Hold in place while slowly pouring more desiccant all around. Be sure to work the drying medium in between every petal and leaf to prevent mildew.

Add as many flowers or sprigs as you wish, but they must not touch each other. Cover each layer with more desiccant. If you are using a deep container, you can add several layers of bloom or foliage. Cover the top layer with an inch or two of the drying compound.

After the container is filled, put on the lid and store it in a warm dry place where it can remain undisturbed until the flowers and leaves dry. Most flowers take 2 to 3 days. In sand they will require 1 to 3 weeks. The faster the material is dried, the better the color retention.

Drying trays are simple to make or can be purchased readymade.

Test the dryness by carefully removing a flower or leaf from the box or jar. It should feel dry and crisp. If not completely dried, return it to the container and cover again.

When dry, remove the blooms or sprigs carefully and gently shake or brush off all the desiccant.

To make stems longer, add any desired length of florist's wire and wrap with floral tape, stretching it as you go. Keep dried blooms out of direct sunlight to hold their color longer.

Glycerin drying. Glycerin-dried rose hips and branches of herbal shrubs such as eucalyptus highlight winter decorations. The natural color will darken but the fragrance remains. The leaves and hips stay soft and supple.

Add one part glycerin (available from drugstores) to two parts very hot water. Put into a tightly closed bottle, shake well to mix, then pour into a saucepan and bring just to the boiling point.

Cut or smash the bottom of foliage stems and place them upright in a container. Pour in the hot glycerin mixture until it reaches about 2 inches up the stems.

Put the container in a warm place with an abundance of natural light. Check the container daily. You will probably need to add more of the heated glycerin solution during the first few days to keep the 2 inches of stem covered.

If you want to vary the naturally dark brown color that results from the glycerin process, add 1 fluid ounce of food coloring for each 3 cups of glycerin solution. The resulting color will depend on how long you leave the herb in the mixture.

Normally it takes 2 to 3 weeks to complete the preserving process. Hips or leaves should be soft and shiny after the water and glycerin have been absorbed by the plant. In time the water evaporates, and the glycerin stays behind in the cells.

It is natural for beads of moisture to appear on the surface of the hips or leaves, especially if the air is humid or the material stays too long in the solution. When this happens remove the stems from the solution and gently wipe or rinse off the excess moisture. Cut away sticky ends.

Freezing. This method is recommended for a few of the tender herbs such as basil, burnet, fennel, tarragon, chives, dill, and parsley. Simply tie a small bundle of the herb together and dip it head-first into boiling water for a few seconds. Cool immediately by plunging it into ice water for a couple of minutes. (The blanching is not necessary for basil, chives, dill or parsley.) Remove the leaves from the stems and put into plastic bags, label, and freeze.

Freezing is a good way to save the herbs that you pick and do not use fresh during the season. Just chop the leaves before freezing and store in small bags, only as much as you will use at one time.

Salt curing. Some of the tender herbs such as basil, burnet, dill, fennel, and parsley can be packed in salt. Wash and drain, remove leaves from their stems, place them in alternate layers with plain table salt in a container, beginning and ending with salt layers. Fill the container completely and cover with an airtight lid. Label and store in a cool dark place. Rinse the salt off the leaves before using.

Packing in vinegar. The French tightly pack tarragon leaves in little jars, then completely fill the jar with vinegar. You might try this method with other leafy herbs as well. Both the herbs and the flavored vinegar can be used.

Preserving onions. Onions may be frozen, canned, pickled, or dried.

To freeze, peel and chop, then store in plastic bags or containers. Use within 3 months.

Above: A garland of garlic dries in the sun.
Opposite: The Shakers still dry their bountiful herb harvests by traditional methods.

To can, peel small onions and boil for 5 minutes in water to which ¾ cup of vinegar has been added. Drain and pack into sterilized jars. Cover with a boiling brine made of ¾-cup vinegar and 3 tablespoons salt to 1 gallon water. Leave ½-inch headroom. Seal and process for 25 minutes in a canner at 10 pounds pressure.

To pickle, follow any pickling recipe: pack, seal, and process.

To dry, peel and slice thinly or chop. Spread in a thin layer on a drying rack. Stir daily until crisp. Store in airtight containers.

To dry whole onions, shallots, or garlic, simply store in a mesh bag or wire basket. You may also make a decorative braid to hang: Leave the stems on the bulbs and clean off ugly leaves and the first skin layer. Braid strands with the remaining leaves beginning with three bulbs, just as you would a pigtail. Continue braiding and adding bulbs. Tie off end with twine. Hang in a dry well-ventilated place. Cut off bulbs and use them as needed.

Preserving peppers. Sweet or hot peppers may be preserved in the same ways as onions.

To freeze, simply wash and halve and remove seeds and pulp. Slice or dice and pack in containers or bags, and freeze. Blanching is not required. Use within 12 months.

To can, cut out stem ends and remove pulp and seeds. Peel by roasting in a hot oven or over an open flame until skins separate. Chill immediately in cold water. Pack into hot, sterilized jars. Add 1 teaspoon salt and 1 tablespoon lemon juice per quart of boiling water and pour to within ½ inch of jar tops, being sure all the pepper is covered. Seal and process in a canner at 5 pounds pressure for 50 minutes (pints) or 60 minutes (quarts).

To pickle, follow directions in any pickling recipe.

To dry, wash the peppers and remove seeds and pulp, slice into thin strips and blanch in boiling water for 10 minutes. Spread in a thin layer on a drying rack. Stir daily until brittle. Store in airtight containers.

To dry whole, start with heavy twine and tie a square knot around the stem of a whole fresh pepper. Continue tying peppers to make a long string. Hang in a dry well-ventilated place. Cut peppers from the string as needed.

Storage and shelf life. To retain their flavor, dried herbs should be kept as whole as possible and stored in airtight containers away from the heat of the stove and moisture. Some people advocate dark jars, cans, or ceramic containers. Clear jars or bottles—even plastic bags—are equally effective as long as they are kept away from the sun or other bright light.

When stored in a cool ventilated place, leafy herbs can be expected to retain their freshness for an entire year. Seeds and roots will keep somewhat longer.

Strings of dried peppers make beautiful, decorative, and tasty gifts.

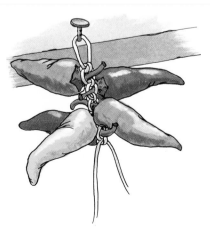

Peppers have short stems and can't be braided like garlic or onions. Use a macramé technique instead. Using a double strand of heavy twine, tie a square knot around the stem of the first pepper and work downward.

Commercially available herbs and spices will last six months or slightly longer before beginning to lose their flavors. They should be stored exactly like homegrown products.

Frozen herbs retain their texture and flavor much longer than one might expect. They will keep indefinitely but are best used within a year. Once they have been thawed, they cannot be refrozen.

A *ristra*, or braid, of chili peppers hangs on an adobe wall in Chimayo, New Mexico. A *ristra* is composed of 2 bushels of freshly harvested chiles.

HERBS AND SPICES IN THE LANDSCAPE

Design an herb garden with a theme in mind. Plant a bed of gray and silver herbs, for example, to contrast with the vivid colors of a flowering border.

If you are inclined to think of herbs in terms of weedy garden plants or a few straggly pots on a kitchen windowsill, you have a pleasant surprise in store. Herbs and spices that are planted with attention to a good sense of design, given proper culture, and kept well groomed can be among the most beautiful plants in the house and garden. The fact that they are useful as flavorings, fragrances, cosmetics, teas, or dyes as well as being ornamental is an added advantage for the gardener. If you need further reasons for adding them to the garden, many herbs resist drought, repel insects, and require little care. This practical aspect combined with their attractiveness makes herbs and spices valuable assets to any landscape.

Many of the herbs grown today as ornamentals were originally valued for medicinal or some other long-forgotten purpose. Gardeners have learned to love them for their historical significance or just for their form, leaf texture, coloration, flowers, or other visual aspects.

Tradition dictates that herbs be relegated to a separate herb garden, either following a formal pattern or planted together informally. You may choose to follow this tradition and reserve one part of your garden for herbs and spices, but you will probably enjoy experimenting with the multitude of herb varieties in all parts of your garden, in containers indoors, or simply alongside other good things to eat in the vegetable garden. Herbs and spices can be part of the total landscape in the modern garden, alongside flowering bulbs and other ornamental annuals, perennials, and shrubs.

Consider some of the ways herbs can be incorporated into the garden. Low-growing herbs such as parsley, chives, dwarf sages, and thymes are often at their best as borders or edging around flowering beds or planted among annuals and perennials in a blooming border. They are a pretty and practical edging for tall perennial flowers and are perfect for filling corners and empty spaces between other plantings. Set out spreading herbs such as chamomile and creeping thyme to form ground covers or fragrant carpeted garden pathways.

Low-growing herbs are attractive combined with the alpines, bulbs, and succulents usually grown in rock gardens and are an excellent landscaping solution for hillsides and slopes. Try plantings of rosemary or creeping thyme to cascade gracefully over terraces of stone, wood, or railroad ties.

Anywhere you want a brilliant spot of color you may plant flowering herbs, purple leaf basil, or tricolor sage. Create a subdued effect with one of the gray foliages such as dittany of Crete or gray santolina. Tuck the plants alongside whatever else is growing in the area, as long as the culture is compatible.

For a shaded wooded area, plant fernlike chervil or sweet cicely. Woodruff, mints, and violets are good company for these shade-tolerant plants as ground cover under trees.

Although the majority of herbs and spices require well-drained soil, a few

can be used in a water garden—whether it be a slow stream, a formally planted pool, a sunken tub, or an oversized container which can even be brought indoors. Four herbs that do well in extremely moist environments are the water chestnut, lotus, sweet flag, and watercress.

Designing an Outdoor Herb Garden

If you wish to follow tradition and have a special garden devoted to herbs, you may elect either a formal or an informal design.

Formal herb gardens were popular during the Middle Ages and are characterized by symmetrical design, often with geometric planting patterns. These planting areas or *parterres* are traditionally bounded with a manicured low edging of boxwood, santolina, or other compact shrub that can be kept shaped and controlled. Bricks, large stones, or strips of weathered wood can also be used as edging.

The formal garden usually features paths of brick, stone, crushed stone, or gravel running in geometrical patterns among the beds. Other good materials for paths include shells or hulls and other organic material indigenous to your area. The focal point of the garden can be a spectacularly tall specimen plant, a birdbath, a fountain, a beehive of twisted straw, or a sundial or other garden sculpture. Planted or empty urns are often placed symmetrically in the garden.

The Elizabethan knot garden was characterized by the famous interwoven knot or ribbon planting. You can choose to duplicate a design steeped in history or create your own version. The accompanying drawing shows one such design, with possible choices of plants to execute it. Work out the planting idea on paper, then transfer it to the garden by setting out wooden stakes and marking off the planting area with stretched string. Use a middle stake with a string to form circles and curves. Choose plant material that can be easily shaped and will stay compact when clipped; sage, bush basil, lemon thyme, spearmint, peppermint, santolina, and boxwood are good candidates. The remaining open areas can be mulched with crushed stones or organic matter to contrast with the living plants and to keep weeds down.

The informal herb garden is free-form with plants irregularly spaced for a natural appearance. Informal designs are typified by the picturesque cottage garden of towering hollyhocks and delphiniums over great clumps of lavenders interplanted with all sorts of foliage and flowers. But there are

Above: A pond or stream is not required to grow water-loving herbs; a tub of water will do. This water garden holds the reedlike water chestnut, the round-leaved lotus, and spicy watercress.

Opposite: The knot garden at the Brooklyn Botanic Gardens is based on the traditional Elizabethan garden. You may plan your own knot garden using the drawing below.

A Knot Garden Design

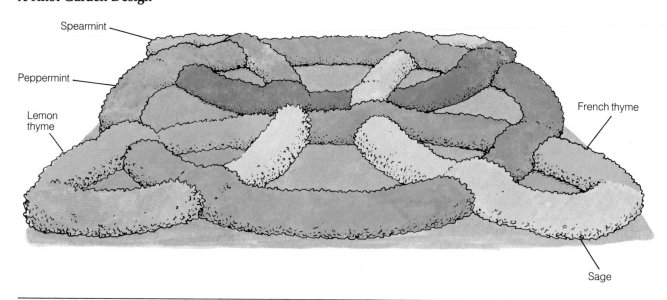

Spearmint

Peppermint

Lemon thyme

French thyme

Sage

An herbal kitchen garden shares its bed with spring bulbs. For continual eye-catching color, summer-flowering annuals can be planted after the daffodil blooms fade.

many other ways to develop informal designs including rock gardens, terraces, raised beds, woodland scenes, and contemporary modular sections devoted to each herb.

Whereas the formal garden utilizes herbs and spices that can be kept under control, the informal garden design relies heavily on rambling herbs such as mints, catnip, lemon balm, scented geraniums, and shrub roses. Informal gardens can also benefit from a few garden accessories casually placed.

No matter what your choice of design, remember to include places to sit among the plants to enjoy their fragrances and beauty. It may be simply a railing or cap on the edge of a raised bed, a weathered wooden bench, or traditional or modern garden furniture.

Whether you choose a formal or informal version of the herb garden, you should use the same procedure in methodically planning your landscape. Begin with a study of garden catalogs and books. Visit public and private gardens to see what you would like to grow and how these plants are placed in the landscape. Many arboreta and public gardens have special sections devoted to herbs. Perhaps you want only culinary plants or just those with memorable fragrances. Many people choose to follow a theme and plant all the herbs mentioned in the Bible or in the writings of Shakespeare, or the herbs that were common to a particular historical period. Other popular themes include native American herbs, lemon-scented foliages, gardens that attract bees, or an herbal tea garden. Lists of plants that might be included in such theme gardens are on pages 49–51.

Give your attention first to the overall form and to the individual shapes you want in your garden. Make a list of plants that can fulfill these requirements, starting with those you really want to grow and adding others that are necessary to satisfy the design.

Rambling herbs interplanted with flowering perennials lend a natural look to this informal herb garden.

Then turn your thoughts to coloring the design. Choose varieties of the plants on your list that bloom or have foliage in the right colors. You may create a full spectrum, or concentrate on particular combinations of colors, or choose flowers or leaves for a monochromatic effect.

Once you have your plant list, check each plant's requirements for light and cultural care to see how you can match them with available sunlight and soil conditions. Divide the plants into groups according to their requirements and plan to group those with like needs together. Herbs are so versatile, however, that the groupings will not have to be strict.

It is important to keep growth habits—such as height and spread—in mind when you determine what to plant where. Common sense dictates planting tall herbs as hedges, backgrounds, or accents and to vary the heights so every plant has a chance to receive sun and air and to be seen. Remember to include some evergreen plants or shrubs in your design to prevent large bare spots in your garden during the winter.

Make a diagram of your garden space on paper and position new beds, plants, paths, and accessories in combination with the existing trees and large shrubs that you want to retain. Then take the diagram to the garden and walk through your idea, making any necessary changes. Now you are ready to plant.

Whenever you plant an herb, especially an unusual one, you will want to include a label. There are wooden, metal, and plastic markers available from nursery suppliers. If you cannot find markers that suit your taste, consider designing your own of wood, slate, or other material to blend into the garden. Some gardeners use wooden cooking spoons, for example, to mark their culinary herbs.

When you plant a new garden, try to be patient—it may take several years for a new garden to mature.

Any garden, especially one planted with herbs that tend to look straggly if unattended, will not retain its original good looks without regular grooming and maintenance. If you do all your own garden maintenance, keep the landscape design simple. If you are a newcomer to gardening, start with only a few common, easily grown herbs that appeal to you; two dozen of these are illustrated on pages 43 and 44. (Their specific requirements are detailed in the Plant Selection Guide.) Learning to grow these well before moving on to others saves disappointment and will build your gardening confidence. As you gain experience, do not be afraid to experiment with new plants, new ways to grow familiar varieties, or innovations in garden design.

Herbs in Containers

Herbs do not have to be confined to a permanent place in the garden. Container-grown plants can be moved about as needed to fill empty spots or to stage instant garden shows on a patio, deck, or terrace. Plants in containers are an obvious choice for those with little or no garden space and, of course, for those gardeners who enjoy creating a living landscape indoors.

A rich and decorative harvest can be grown in a small space using suspended containers and pots.

PPLE MINT

LAVENDER

SPEARMINT

OMMON THYME

COSTMARY

LEMON THYME

ANSY

VARIEGATED SAGE

YARROW

REGANO

PEPPERMINT

PINEAPPLE SAGE

GOLDEN SAGE

HYSSOP

GARDEN SAGE

SILVER THYME

SOUTHERNWOOD

PENNYROYAL

DITTANY OF CRETE

CARAWAY

CATNIP

CORIANDER

ORANGE BERGAMOT MINT

PARSLEY

The container. Although many people prefer the natural look of clay pots, any type of container that has good drainage and enough room for the plant's roots can be used.

Among the more popular containers for herbs are plastic pots, all one color or mixed according to their setting. Remember that plants in plastic containers need watering only about a third as often as those in clay pots because the plastic is not porous and the soil retains moisture far longer.

You can adapt any kind of container to herb growing, so there is no need to limit yourself to traditional pots. Consider clear Lucite in cubes or other geometric shapes, colorful glazed ceramics, wooden planters and tubs and half-barrels, clay strawberry jars, coffee canisters and other kitchen cans. There are flats and wooden trays, racks to hold 4-inch pots—soda pop cartons will do—wire baskets, wicker baskets with metal or plastic liners, and hanging containers in many designs.

There are many containers from which to choose, so there is no excuse for planting in one that has no drainage, no matter how pretty it looks. It makes watering too complicated and is unhealthy for your plant. Save such a container for water plants, rooting cuttings, or cut flowers, or plant in a pot that drains and will fit inside the container.

Container gardening outdoors. Container gardening gives you the freedom to position plants at eye-level or—perhaps more importantly with many herbs and spices—at nose-level. Suspend plants in baskets or hanging pots from roof overhangs, tree branches, or posts. Flat-sided wire baskets of herbs and spices can hang on fences, walls or any similar surface. Plant trailing rosemary and thyme to spill out of window boxes, or combine these plantings with upright herbs and vegetables.

Plant different herbs with a common denominator in the same container (providing their cultural requirements are the same). Some variations might include a basket of spaghetti sauce herbs; collections of one species of plant with several varieties, such as thyme; a tub of assorted mints for teas; planters of your favorite *bouquet garni* herbs; or a mixture of lettuce and other salad greens with herbs that will end up in the same bowl.

The adventuresome gardener can try a hand at special shapes. Dig older plants with woody stems such as oregano and rosemary from the garden, put them in pots, trim them, and train them to grow as bonsai. Remove the side shoots along a single woody upright stem and shape the foliage at the top as a tree or standard. Prune and train boxwood, myrtle, or any compact woody herb into geometric or whimsical topiary shapes.

It's convenient to keep a few culinary herbs near the kitchen door. If there is no garden space, grow them in large tubs or terracotta strawberry jars. That these plantings are utilitarian does not prevent you from planting these containers in an attractive manner. Combine herbs with edible flowers or with those that you will use as table decorations.

A collection of herbs can be grown in small spaces. A few half-buried cement blocks with plantings in the open areas will provide a small harvest. Remove a few bricks from a patio or wide walkway and add herb plants in the holes, or plant creeping herbs between paving stones. If you have only a balcony, deck, or narrow gardening area, go vertical with the planting design. Add shelves, a ladder, stairsteps, or stack wooden or wire boxes to display potted herbs in limited space.

A vertical garden of herbs can flourish with a simple homemade box. Build it as tall and wide as you like but shallow from front to back—no more than about 12 inches. The narrow ends should be solid board but the wide sides are made by crisscrossing slats nailed to the box at 6-inch intervals. Drill drain holes in the bottom. Line the entire insides of the box with heavy-duty plastic sheeting (punch holes for drainage in the bottom). Secure vertically 2-inch plastic tubes riddled with 1/4-inch holes to use for watering and fill with a lightweight growing medium. Then snip holes in

A flat-sided wire basket holds a combination of herbs used in spaghetti sauce.

Containers range from ceramic strawberry jars (above) to bleached wood trays (below).

Children often come up with creative container ideas for small herb plants.

In a small area, stacked weathered wooden boxes provide a multilevel display for potted herbs, candytuft, and daffodils.

the plastic between the slats and insert roots of young plants. As the herbs grow they will cover the plastic and you will soon have an outdoor living screen or divider.

A wire pole filled with sphagnum moss and growing medium can be planted just like the hanging basket described and illustrated on page 22. If you make one side flat it can be hung or pushed against a wall to conserve gardening space.

Container gardening indoors. If your landscape is limited to the indoors, foremost consideration must be given to meeting the cultural requirements. It is often not possible just to put plants where they will look pretty or where you would like a bit of greenery. A check of available sunlight usually defines the space you have for herb gardening, unless you add sufficient artificial lighting (see page 23) to meet the requirements of most herbs and spices.

For a successful interior landscape choose containers in colors and materials that fit the interior design of the room they will occupy. Classic clay goes with everything.

Remember to put the right type of saucer or tray under indoor containers. Moisture seeping through unglazed clay can damage tabletops and floors, so it is preferable to use glazed clay, plastic, glass, rubber, china, or other nonporous saucers. A layer of small pebbles in the saucer will keep the container's drainage holes above water and provide extra humidity for your plants at the same time.

Group plants indoors just as you would arrange an outdoor flower bed, with tall plants as backgrounds for lower-growing species or as accents among a group of shorter plants. Blend herbs with more traditional tropical house plants and flowering species. Utilize trailing herbs to soften the hard-edged look of shelves, tabletops, or windowsills. Group hanging herbs in the sun on different levels to create a visually pleasing design of suspended forms. Choose hardware for hanging with attention to the design and what looks best in the room.

Planting in containers offers the convenience of being able to bring outdoor plants indoors and vice versa. Remember though that such a change in environment can be a shock to a plant. Generally, plants adapt more readily to changes from indoors to outdoors than the other way around. Younger

Vertical Garden on Wheels

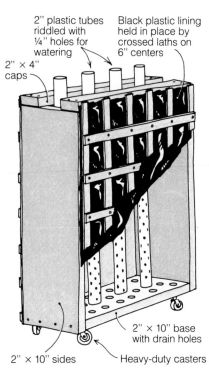

2" plastic tubes riddled with ¼" holes for watering

Black plastic lining held in place by crossed laths on 6" centers

2" × 4" caps

2" × 10" base with drain holes

2" × 10" sides

Heavy-duty casters

Fill with soil mix. Cut holes through plastic to insert small plants.

plants will adapt more easily to changes in environment than older plants; the smaller plants may look a little droopy for a while, but if you provide them with attentive care, they will most often revive. Plants transferred indoors for a short period, such as a day or two, will probably show no ill effects.

The key to making the most of herbs and spices, whether indoors or in the outdoor garden, is a new appreciation of the plant itself. Look at it for its visual contributions to the garden as well as the many ways to use the harvest of flowers, leaves, stems, seeds, and roots. Keep the plants looking healthy and vigorous by learning all you can about how to grow them.

Herb Garden Themes

In the tradition of the great European and English gardens, you may wish to design an herb garden around a specific theme. Of course, just creating an herb garden is in itself a theme—using the utilitarian herbs and spices and those of historical interest (such as boxwood, hollyhocks, or hen-and-chickens) as plant materials.

Reading through the following lists, you will notice that many plants are included in two or three or more lists. Considering the versatility of most herbs, this is not surprising. A plant may be included in one of the historical themes such as the Shakespeare garden or medieval garden; the unique oil produced by a plant that guarantees its inclusion in the cook's garden also insures that it will be included in the fragrance garden and the tea garden.

Depending on the size of your garden, you may wish to explore more than one of these themes, allotting, for example, culinary herbs to one bed, gray and silver herbs to another, and flowering herbs to a third. Many herbs have generally the same requirements for sun, soil, and water, but others do not. Check the cultural requirements of each herb you might wish to plant in the Plant Selection Guide on pages 96–127.

Food-tin containers add a touch of color to a small herb garden on a sunny kitchen windowsill, which provides fresh herbs for the cook.

With each common name of an herb or spice we have given the botanical name in parentheses. Many plants, especially those in use for centuries, have accumulated several different common names, but in each of the languages used in all the countries where they are known, there is only one correct botanical name, which is the same everywhere. The first name is that of the *genus*; and the second name, when combined with the genus, is the *species*. When the common name covers more than one species, we have listed just the genus; some of the species within these genera are given in the Plant Selection Guide.

Opposite: In the Shakespeare Garden at the Huntington Library Gardens in San Marino, California, a bust of the playwright is set among decorative beds filled with the herbs mentioned in his works.

Shakespeare Garden

The following are nonpoisonous herbs mentioned in the writings of William Shakespeare. All were popular in Elizabethan England.

Bay (*Laurus nobilis*)
Burnet (*Poterium sanguisorba*)
Calendula (*Calendula officinalis*)
Carnation (*Dianthus* species)
Chamomile (*Chamaemelum nobile*)
Dyer's broom (*Genista tinctoria*)
Hyssop (*Hyssopus officinalis*)
Johnny-jump-up (*Viola tricolor*)
Lavender (*Lavandula* species)
Lemon balm (*Melissa officinalis*)
Marjoram (*Origanum majorana*)
Mint (*Mentha* species)
Mustard (*Brassica* species)
Myrtle (*Myrtus communis*)
Parsley (*Petroselinum crispum*)
Pink (*Dianthus* species)
Rose (*Rosa* species)
Rosemary (*Rosmarinus officinalis*)
Savory (*Satureja* species)
Strawberry (*Fragaria vesca*)
Thyme (*Thymus* species)

Good Cook's Garden

Most of the plants on this list are favorite ingredients in the kitchen. You may want to plant a selection of them near the kitchen door to save steps.

Angelica (*Angelica* species)
Anise (*Pimpinella anisum*)
Basil (*Ocimum basilicum*)
Bay (*Laurus nobilis*)
Borage (*Borago officinalis*)
Burnet (*Poterium sanguisorba*)
Caraway (*Carum carvi*)
Chervil (*Anthriscus cerefolium*)
Chives (*Allium schoenoprasum*)
Garland chrysanthemum (*Chrysanthemum coronarium*)
Coriander (*Coriandrum sativum*)
Costmary (*Chrysanthemum balsamita*)
Cumin (*Cuminum cyminum*)
Dill (*Anethum graveolens*)
Garlic (*Allium sativum*)
Horehound (*Marrubium vulgare*)
Horseradish (*Armoracia rusticana*)
Hyssop (*Hyssopus officinalis*)
Lavender (*Lavandula* species)
Leek (*Allium ampeloprasum*)
Lovage (*Levisticum officinale*)
Marjoram (*Origanum majorana*)
Mint (*Mentha* species)
Mustard (*Brassica* species)
Nasturtium (*Tropaeolum* species)
Onion (*Allium cepa*)
Oregano (*Origanum vulgare*)

Parsley (*Petroselinum crispum*)
Chili peppers (*Capsicum annuum*)
Rocket (*Eruca vesicaria* subspecies *sativa*)
Rose (*Rosa* species)
Rosemary (*Rosmarinus officinalis*)
Sage (*Salvia* species)
Savory (*Satureja* species)
Sesame (*Sesamum indicum*)
Shallot (*Allium cepa*)
Sorel (*Rumex* species)
Tarragon (*Artemisia dracunculus*)
Watercress (*Nasturtium officinale*)

Medieval Garden

Among the many plants protected within walled monastery gardens of the Middle Ages are these herbs, still used and enjoyed centuries later.

Angelica (*Angelica* species)
Caraway (*Carum carvi*)
Chives (*Allium schoenoprasum*)
Iris (*Iris* species)
Johnny-jump-up (*Viola tricolor*)
Lavender (*Lavandula* species)
Lemon balm (*Melissa officinalis*)
Marjoram (*Origanum majorana*)
Mint (*Mentha* species)
Pink (*Dianthus* species)
Rose (*Rosa* species)
Rosemary (*Rosmarinus officinalis*)
Sage (*Salvia* species)
Santolina (*Santolina* species)
Shallot (*Allium cepa*)
Southernwood (*Artemisia abrotanum*)
Strawberry (*Fragaria vesca*)

Bee Garden

A garden composed of these plants that are attractive to bees will be a special delight to gardeners who are beekeepers or those who just enjoy the buzzing on a summer's day.

Basil (*Ocimum basilicum*)
Bergamot (*Monarda punctata*)
Borage (*Borago officinalis*)
Catnip (*Nepeta cataria*)
Chamomile (*Chamaemelum nobile*)
Fennel (*Foeniculum vulgare*)
Germander (*Teucrium chamaedrys*)
Horehound (*Marrubium vulgare*)
Hyssop (*Hyssopus officinalis*)
Lavender (*Lavandula* species)
Lemon balm (*Melissa officinalis*)
Linden (*Tilia* species)
Marjoram (*Origanum majorana*)
Oregano (*Origanum vulgare*)
Rosemary (*Rosmarinus officinalis*)
Sage (*Salvia* species)
Savory, winter (*Satureja montana*)
Sweet cicely (*Myrrhis odorata*)
Thyme (*Thymus* species)

A tea garden can provide tea made from a single herb or a blend of several, with flowers or spices added for fragrance and flavor.

The Flowering Garden

A well-planned garden of herbs and spices can provide many flowers for fragrances cutting, drying, eating, garnishing, or just enjoying. Many herbs other than the ones listed here flower, but some should be harvested just before their flowers bloom.

Angelica (*Angelica* species)
Anise (*Pimpinella anisum*)
Bergamot (*Monarda didyma*)
Borage (*Borago officinalis*)
Calendula (*Calendula officinalis*)
Carnation (*Dianthus caryophyllus*)
Chamomile (*Chamaemelum nobile*)
Chervil (*Anthriscus cerefolium*)
Garland chrysanthemum (*Chrysanthemum coronarium*)
Coriander (*Coriandrum sativum*)
Cornflower (*Centaurea cyanus*)
Costmary (*Chrysanthemum balsamita*)
Cumin (*Cuminum cyminum*)
Dandelion (*Taraxacum officinale*)
Dill (*Anethum graveolens*)
Elecampane (*Inula helenium*)
Fennel flower (*Nigella sativa*)
Foxglove (*Digitalis purpurea*)
Geraniums, scented (*Pelargonium* species)
Ginger (*Zingiber officinale*)
Goldenrod (*Solidago odora*)
Great mullein (*Verbascum thapsus*)
Heliotrope (*Heliotropium arborescens*)
Hibiscus (*Hibiscus rosa-sinensis*)
Hollyhock (*Alcea rosea*)
Hyssop (*Hyssopus officinalis*)
Johnny-jump-up (*Viola tricolor*)
Lavender (*Lavandula* species)
Lily-of-the-valley (*Convallaria majalis*)
Lovage (*Levisticum officinale*)
Marsh mallow (*Althaea officinalis*)
Mustard (*Brassica* species)
Pink (*Dianthus* species)

Rose (*Rosa* species)
Rosemary (*Rosmarinus officinalis*)
Safflower (*Carthamus tinctorius*)
Saffron crocus (*Crocus sativus*)
Sunflower (*Helianthus annuus*)
Tansy (*Tanacetum vulgare*)
Thyme (*Thymus* species)
Valerian (*Valeriana officinalis*)
Violet (*Viola odorata*)
Wood betony (*Stachys officinalis*)
Woodruff (*Galium odoratum*)
Yarrow (*Achillea millefolium*)

Tea Garden

Almost every herb and spice can be made into a tea. The following examples are especially good and will make an attractive planting as well. For directions on how to brew herbal teas, see page 74.

Angelica (*Angelica* species)
Basil (*Ocimum basilicum*)
Bergamot (*Monarda* species)
Borage (*Borago officinalis*)
Catnip (*Nepeta cataria*)
Chamomile (*Chamaemelum nobile*)
Costmary (*Chrysanthemum balsamita*)
Dill (*Anethum graveolens*)
Fennel (*Foeniculum vulgare*)
Goldenrod (*Solidago odora*)
Hibiscus (*Hibiscus rosa-sinensis*)
Horehound (*Marrubium vulgare*)
Jasmine (*Jasminum* species)
Lemon balm (*Melissa officinalis*)
Lemon verbena (*Aloysia triphylla*)
Lovage (*Levisticum officinale*)
Marjoram (*Origanum majorana*)
Mint (*Mentha* species)
Parsley (*Petroselinum crispum*)
Rose (*Rosa* species)
Rosemary (*Rosmarinus officinalis*)

Sage (*Salvia* species)
Sassafras (*Sassafras albidum*)
Speedwell (*Veronica officinalis*)
Strawberry (*Fragaria vesca*)
Sweet cicely (*Myrrhis odorata*)
Tansy (*Tanacetum vulgare*)
Thyme (*Thymus* species)
Wood betony (*Stachys officinalis*)
Woodruff (*Galium odoratum*)

Dyer's Garden

Among the many plants used as natural dyes, these additionally make pleasurable additions to the landscape. Refer to page 94 for the colors produced by some of these plants.

Agrimony (*Agrimonia eupatoria*)
Ajuga (*Ajuga reptans*)
Alkanet (*Anchusa officinalis*)
Birch (*Betula* species)
Blackberry (*Rubus* species)
Bloodroot (*Sanguinaria canadensis*)
Calendula (*Calendula officinalis*)
Cornflower (*Centaurea cyanus*)
Dandelion (*Taraxacum officinale*)
Dyer's broom (*Genista tinctoria*)
Elecampane (*Inula helenium*)
Goldenrod (*Solidago odora*)
Hibiscus (*Hibiscus rosa-sinensis*)
Hollyhock (*Alcea rosea*)
Hyssop (*Hyssopus officinalis*)
Indigo, false (*Baptisia tinctoria*)
Juniper (*Juniperus communis*)
Lady's mantle (*Alchemilla vulgaris*)
Lily-of-the-valley (*Convallaria majalis*)
Onion (*Allium cepa*)
Parsley (*Petroselinum crispum*)
Safflower (*Carthamus tinctorius*)
Sassafras (*Sassafras albidum*)
Sorrel (*Rumex* species)
Sumac (*Rhus glabra*)
Sunflower (*Helianthus annuus*)
Tansy (*Tanacetum vulgare*)
Turmeric (*Curcuma domestica*)
Violet (*Viola odorata*)
Yarrow (*Achillea millefolium*)

Garden of Fragrances

A walk through a garden designed for fragrances is a delight to all the senses. Not only are the smells of the flowers and foliage captivating, but the plants are visually pleasing and tastily refreshing.

Angelica (*Angelica* species)
Basil (*Ocimum basilicum*)
Bayberry (*Myrica pensylvanica*)
Bergamot (*Monarda* species)
Burnet (*Poterium sanguisorba*)
Catnip (*Nepeta cataria*)
Chamomile (*Chamaemelum nobile*)
Costmary (*Chrysanthemum balsamita*)
Eucalyptus (*Eucalyptus* species)
Gas plant (*Dictamnus albus*)
Geraniums, scented (*Pelargonium* species)
Good-King-Henry (*Chenopodium bonus-henricus*)
Heliotrope (*Heliotropium arborescens*)
Hyssop (*Hyssopus officinalis*)
Jasmine (*Jasminum* species)
Lavender (*Lavandula* species)
Lemon balm (*Melissa officinalis*)
Lemon verbena (*Aloysia triphylla*)
Lily-of-the-valley (*Convallaria majalis*)
Marjoram (*Origanum majorana*)
Mint (*Mentha* species)
Oregano (*Origanum vulgare*)

Pennyroyal (*Mentha pulegium*)
Rose (*Rosa* species)
Rosemary (*Rosmarinus officinalis*)
Sage (*Salvia* species)
Savory (*Satureja* species)
Southernwood (*Artemisia abrotanum*)
Sweet cicely (*Myrrhis odorata*)
Sweet flag (*Acorus calamus*)
Sweet olive (*Osmanthus fragrans*)
Tansy (*Tanacetum vulgare*)
Tarragon (*Artemisia dracunculus*)
Thyme (*Thymus* species)
Valerian (*Valeriana officinalis*)
Violet (*Viola odorata*)
Woodruff (*Galium odoratum*)
Yarrow (*Achillea millefolium*)

Gray and Silver Garden

A monochromatic gray and silver garden is an old tradition in English gardens. A quiet place of subtle shimmering foliages is a pleasant place to visit, especially on a moonlit evening. Gray foliage highlights the colors of the flowers of these plants and provides a contrast to other vivid flower beds. Many of these plants are also fragrant.

Apple mint (*Mentha suaveolens*)
Carnation (*Dianthus caryophyllus*)
Catnip (*Nepeta cataria*)
Clary sage (*Salvia sclarea*)
Germander (*Teucrium chamaedrys*)
Gray sage (*Salvia leucophylla*)
Gray santolina (*Santolina chamaecyparissus*)
Great mullein (*Verbascum thapsus*)
Horehound (*Marrubium vulgare*)
Lamb's ears (*Stachys byzantina*)
Lavender (*Lavandula angustifolia*)
Marsh mallow (*Althaea officinalis*)
Nutmeg geranium (*Pelargonium* × *fragrans*)
Oregano (*Origanum vulgare*)
Pineapple mint (*Mentha suaveolens* 'Variegata')
Rosemary (*Rosmarinus officinalis*)
Silver sage (*Salvia argentea*)
Silver tansy (*Tanacetum compactum*)
Silver thyme (*Thymus vulgaris* 'Argentus')
Southernwood (*Artemisia abrotanum*)
Yarrow (*Achillea millefolium*)

A gray-and-silver garden, favorite of many flower gardeners, can be filled with fragrant herbs. Low-growing gray lavender cotton (*Santolina chamaecyparissus*) edges a silvery bed backed by pygmy barberry and the taller gray lamb's ears (*Stachys* species).

Landscaping Categories

In addition to the themes that can guide your selection of plants, you must also consider the growth habits and cultural requirements of the plants, or the specific functions you wish the plants to perform in your landscape. If part of your garden is in the shade, for example, you will have to limit the plants you place there to those that need little sun. Or, to simplify your garden chores, you may wish to plant those herbs and spices that need to be kept moist in a different bed from those that need little water. Along the same lines, if you wish certain plants to function as a hedge in your garden, you need a plant that can be clipped and shaped and that will not grow too quickly.

The fact that any two plants are in the same category does not mean they can be grown together. For example, both lily-of-the-valley and marsh mallow prefer their soil to be kept moist, but lily-of-the-valley likes a shady exposure and marsh mallow likes full sun. These lists are only intended to provided *general* categories to help you plan your garden; refer to the Plant Selection Guide on pages 96–127 for the complete description of cultural requirements and growth habits of each plant.

Plants That Like Full or Partial Shade

This list enumerates only those plants that *prefer* full or partial shade. Many plants that flourish in full sun will also adapt to partial shade; they are *not* included here. Plant names followed by an asterisk (*) like full shade, the others prefer partial shade.

Angelica (*Angelica* species)
Bloodroot (*Sanguinaria canadensis*)*
Chervil (*Anthricus cerefolium*)
Comfrey (*Symphytum officinale*)*
Ginger (*Zingiber officinale*)
Ginseng (*Panax quinquefolius*)*
Lily-of-the-valley (*Convallaria majalis*)*
Mint (*Mentha* species)
Parsley (*Petroselinum crispum*)
St.-John's-wort (*Hypericum* species)
Speedwell (*Veronica officinalis*)*
Strawberry, woodland (*Fragaria vesca*)
Sweet cicely (*Myrrhis odorata*)
Sweet olive (*Osmanthus fragrans*)
Tea (*Camellia sinensis*)
Vanilla (*Vanilla planifolia*)
Violet (*Viola odorata*)
Wood betony (*Stachys officinalis*)
Woodruff (*Galium odoratum*)

Plants That Like Moist Soil

The soil around these plants should not be allowed to dry out. Many of these plants require well-draining soil; the soil should be retentive of moisture, but not saturated.

Arrowroot (*Maranta arundinacea*)
Bergamot (*Monarda* species)
Birch (*Betula* species)
Boneset (*Eupatorium perfoliatum*)
Catnip (*Nepeta cataria*)
Chamomile (*Chamaemelum nobile*)
Comfrey (*Symphytum officinalis*)
Elder (*Sambucus canadensis*)
Ginger (*Zingiber officinale*)
Ginseng (*Panax quinquefolius*)
Heliotrope (*Heliotropium arborescens*)
Hops (*Humulus lupulus*)
Horseradish (*Armoracia rusticana*)
Juniper (*Juniperus communis*)
Licorice (*Glycyrrhiza glabra*)
Lily-of-the-valley (*Convallaria majalis*)
Lovage (*Levisticum officinale*)

Marsh mallow (*Althaea officinalis*)
Mint (*Mentha* species)
Parsley (*Petroselinum crispum*)
Sweet cicely (*Myrrhis odorata*)
Sweet flag (*Acorus calamus*)
Turmeric (*Curcuma domestica*)
Vanilla (*Vanilla planifolia*)
Vervain (*Verbena canadensis*)
Violet (*Viola odorata*)
Witch hazel (*Hamamelis virginiana*)
Wood betony (*Stachys officinalis*)
Woodruff (*Galium odoratum*)

Water Garden Plants

These plants like to be planted either directly in water or in soil that is kept saturated with water.

Lotus (*Nelumbo* species)
Sweet flag (*Acorus calamus*)
Water chestnut (*Eleocharis dulcis*)
Watercress (*Nasturtium officinale*)

Plants That Like Dry Soil

Though some are drought-tolerant, the plants in this list cannot be ignored completely. They still need water, but you may allow the soil to dry out between waterings. Remember also that plants transplanted into the garden initially need extra care and attention until they become established.

Agrimony (*Agrimonia eupatoria*)
Artemisia (*Artemisia* species)
Burnet (*Poterium sanguisorba*)
Caper bush (*Capparis spinosa*)
Caraway (*Carum carvi*)
Carob (*Ceratonia siliqua*)
Dittany of Crete (*Origanum dictamnus*)
Dyer's broom (*Genista tinctoria*)
Eucalyptus (*Eucalyptus* species)
Goldenrod (*Solidago odora*)
Great mullein (*Verbascum thapsus*)
Horehound (*Marrubium vulgare*)
Lavender (*Lavandula* species)
Lemon balm (*Melissa officinalis*)
Sage (*Salvia* species)
Santolina (*Santolina* species)
Speedwell (*Veronica officinalis*)
Sumac (*Rhus glabra*)
Yarrow (*Achillea millefolium*)

Heliotrope (*Heliotropium arborescens*), which thrives in moist, well-drained soil, releases a powerful, sweet scent. The English call it "cherry pie plant"; others say the fragrance resembles vanilla.

Size and growth habits

You may find a plant in more than one category because different species or varieties have differing growth habits. Some plants may also be controlled in how they grow by pruning.

Trees

Bay (*Laurus nobilis*)
Birch (*Betula* species)
Carob (*Ceratonia siliqua*)
Red cedar (*Juniperus virginiana*)
Eucalyptus (*Eucalyptus* species)
Juniper (*Juniperus communis*)
Linden (*Tilia* species)
Pomegranate (*Punica granatum*)
Sassafras (*Sassafras albidum*)
Star anise (*Illicium verum*)

Vines

Hops (*Humulus lupulus*)
Jasmine (*Jasminum* species)
Passionflower (*Passiflora incarnata*)
Vanilla (*Vanilla planifolia*)

Large Shrubs

Barberry (*Berberis vulgaris*)
Bay (*Laurus nobilis*)
Bayberry (*Myrica pensylvanica*)
Red cedar (*Juniperus virginiana*)
Coffee (*Coffea arabica*)
Dyer's broom (*Genista tinctoria*)
Elder (*Sambucus canadensis*)
Jasmine (*Jasminum odoratissimum*)
Juniper (*Juniperus communis*)
Myrtle (*Myrtus communis*)
St.-John's-wort (*Hypericum hookeranum*)
Sumac (*Rhus glabra*)
Sweet olive (*Osmanthus fragrans*)
Tea (*Camellia sinensis*)
Witch hazel (*Hamamelis virginiana*)

Ground Covers

Ajuga (*Ajuga reptans*)
Bedstraw (*Galium verum*)
Catnip (*Nepeta cataria*)
Chamomile (*Chamaemelum nobile*)
Germander (*Teucrium chamaedrys*)
Juniper (*Juniperus communis*)
Lamb's ears (*Stachys byzantina*)
Lily-of-the-valley (*Convallaria majalis*)
Mint (*Mentha* species)
Rosemary (*Rosmarinus officinalis* 'Prostratus')
St.-John's-wort (*Hypericum calycinum*)
Santolina (*Santolina* species)
Strawberry, woodland (*Fragaria vesca*)
Thyme (*Thymus serpyllum, T. herba-barona*)
Violet (*Viola odorata*)
Woodruff (*Galium odoratum*)

Specialized landscaping uses

The following two lists offer suggestions of plants that can fulfill the specialized uses of hedges and edgings or low borders in the garden.

Hedges

Angelica (*Angelica* species)
Barberry (*Berberis vulgaris*)
Bergamot (*Monarda* species)
Boxwood (*Buxus* species)
Costmary (*Chrysanthemum balsamita*)
Germander (*Teucrium chamaedrys*)
Hyssop (*Hyssopus officinalis*)
Lovage (*Levisticum officinale*)
Oregano (*Origanum vulgare*)
Sweetbriar rose (*Rosa eglanteria*)
Rosemary (*Rosmarinus officinalis*)
Pineapple sage (*Salvia elegans*)
Tansy (*Tanacetum vulgare*)

Low Borders and Edging

Bush basil (*Ocimum basilicum* 'Minimum')
Chamomile (*Chamaemelum nobile*)
Chives (*Allium schoenoprasum*)
Cumin (*Cuminum cyminum*)
Dittany of Crete (*Origanum dictamnus*)
Lady's mantle (*Alchemilla vulgaris*)
Parsley (*Petroselinum crispum*)
Santolina (*Santolina chamaecyparissus*)
Thyme (*Thymus vulgaris*)

An Indoor Garden

When you plan an indoor herb and spice garden, start with some of these easy-to-grow plants.

Aloe (*Aloe barbadensis*)
Basil (*Ocimum basilicum*)
Bay (*Laurus nobilis*)
Borage (*Borago officinalis*)
Burnet (*Poterium sanguisorba*)
Chervil (*Anthriscus cerefolium*)
Chives (*Allium schoenoprasum*)
Dill (*Anethum graveolens*)
Dittany of Crete (*Origanum dictamnus*)
Fennel (*Foeniculum vulgare*)
Geraniums, scented (*Pelargonium* species)
Ginger (*Zingiber officinale*)
Hyssop (*Hyssopus officinalis*)
Lemon balm (*Melissa officinalis*)
Lemon verbena (*Aloysia triphylla*)
Lovage (*Levisticum officinale*)
Marjoram (*Origanum majorana*)
Mint (*Mentha* species)
Oregano (*Origanum vulgare*)
Parsley (*Petroselinum crispum*)
Pennyroyal (*Mentha pulegium*)
Rosemary (*Rosmarinus officinalis*)
Sage (*Salvia* species)
Savory (*Satureja* species)
Sorrel (*Rumex* species)
Sweet olive (*Osmanthus fragrans*)
Tarragon (*Artemisia dracunculus*)
Thyme (*Thymus* species)

Basil (*Ocimum basilicum*), a native of India, is richly symbolic. The Hindus saw it as a protecting spirit of the family, the Italians as the spirit of love, and the Greeks as a symbol of hate and misfortune. The Romans, who saw basil as a "do-the-opposite" plant, cursed it at planting to make it grow.

CULINARY HERBS AND SPICES

Bake an aromatic herbal bread, blend a spicy condiment, or brew a soothing herbal tea. Herbs and spices invite variety into the kitchen.

Throughout history people have found innumerable ways to use herbs and spices. In various forms they have been used as medicines, decoctions, salves, balms, and ointments to treat every known physical and mental problem. They have been prescribed to induce sleep, to cast enchanted spells, or to drive away serpents and vampires.

Many people now grow or buy herbs for their reported healing or soothing properties. Many volumes have been written on the subject of herbal medications and home remedies. Herbalists list plants to cure almost any ailment.

When it comes to self-diagnosis and self-prescription there can be genuine dangers in herbal remedies, especially for the novice. In the past, herbs that are ineffectual or outright poisonous have been used as treatments for everything from snakebite to cancer.

Nothing in this book is intended to be diagnostic or prescriptive. Any references to medicinal use are historical only, and we assume no responsibility for the use any reader might make of any herb or spice. The omission of herbs and spices that could be poisonous is deliberate. As with all organic material, some herbs and spices can cause allergic reactions in some individuals. Should this happen to you, consult a physician.

This book deals only with the appearance, aroma, and flavor of herbs and spices, and this chapter explores how you can use them in cooking. The next chapter discusses the uses of herbs and spices for their fragrances and in creating cosmetics, crafts, and decorations.

No doubt the use of herbs and spices in cooking claims the attention of more people than any of the other ways these special plants are used. In the past decade American cooks have become routinely acquainted with seasonings previously known only to accomplished chefs. People are still rediscovering many of the wonderful flavors used for generations prior to 20th-century convenience foods.

Herbs and spices should be used to accent and enhance the flavors of foods, not to mask and overwhelm other ingredients. Perhaps a word of caution is in order to cooks just discovering the world of spices. Practice a little restraint, be careful not to overseason. Not every dish needs herbs or spices. But how bland many dishes would be without seasonings! Can you imagine salads, soups, sauces, or stews without herbs and spices? These essential seasonings can transform the simplest foods into rare treats. A few minced herbs added to canned soups lets the busy cook appear to be a genius at serving time.

Learn to be creative with your herbs and spices. Experiment to find flavors and quantities you enjoy. Begin with small amounts and increase as necessary; the degree of seasoning is a matter of personal preference. As you read many of the suggestions and recipes that follow you will note instances where no specific measurement for herbs and spices is given. Quantities must be determined according to your own taste.

Stoveside herbs and spices are most apt to find their way into the cooking pot. Keep them—both fresh and preserved—within easy reach.

When you find a combination of herbs and spices you enjoy, be careful not to become monotonous and repeat the same seasonings over and over. Today you have available spices from all over the world. Often a simple change only in the seasoning will result in an entirely new dish.

Most complete cookbooks have tables, charts, or guides for using herbs and spices with various foods, from appetizers to desserts. Use these guidelines as handy references for basic ideas, but again, do not limit your creativity to another cook's suggestions.

Stoveside herbs. The creative cook will want to have herbs and spices within arm's reach for inspired last-minute additions to foods under preparation.

Keep a small pottery or porcelain pot near the stove. Add whatever sprigs or leaves are left over from daily herb harvest and uses. Reach into the herb pot for a pinch to add as you cook. The flavor will never remain constant as the herb mixture varies from day to day.

You might also enjoy hanging small bunches of drying herbs near the stove to use as needed. They will have a useful life of only a couple of months as their flavor is rapidly lost when exposed to air and heat. Festive strands of dried peppers, garlic, and onions last longer than herbs.

Kitchen equipment. The well-equipped kitchen should have a mortar and pestle for grinding and blending herbs and seeds. This utilitarian tool can be of wood, ceramic, stone, or metal. Most cooks favor wood, but the choice is really a matter of personal taste.

Keep a sharp knife and a pair of kitchen scissors handy for mincing fresh herbs, or chop them on a wooden board. Other items you will want to have on hand include a nutmeg grater with a storage top for unused portions of the whole nutmegs; mills for grinding white and black peppercorns; other grinding mills for whole spices such as allspice and cloves and herb seeds; a press for garlic; perhaps a special grinder for sesame seeds (available from oriental food markets); and cheesecloth and string, or a fine wire mesh tea ball for making *bouquets garnis* (see page 60).

You can get along without any of these items, of course, but they make your use of herbs and spices more enjoyable and efficient.

Using Fresh Herbs

Gather herbs from the garden as you need them. (Be sure they have not been exposed to any sprays or insecticides.) Wash them quickly in cold water when you bring them in and discard any bad leaves. Keep garden or produce-market herbs crisp for several days by storing them in sealed plastic bags or containers in the refrigerator.

Mince or chop small amounts as you need them. Flavors are quickly lost when volatile oils are released by heat. Add herbs to hot dishes at the last minute, unless you are preparing a simmering stock.

If a recipe calls for cooking fresh leafy herbs in oil or butter and then browning meat in the same pan, reverse the order. Brown the meat, then add the fresh herbs. Otherwise the delicate leaves will be fried crisp, brown, and undistinguishable.

The inventive cook uses graters, grinders, presses, strainers, and snippers to prepare herbs and spices for kitchen use.

Invite guests to garnish a salad or soup with snips from an herb garden centerpiece. Nasturtium flowers and leaves add a pungent flavor.

Fresh herbs on the table. The creative cook knows that there are other herbs besides parsley to use for garnishes. Look for color among your herb varieties: sprigs of purple basil, shisho, lemon thyme, or tricolor sage. Add a garland of rosemary in bloom around a crown roast. Or make a wreath of watercress accented with brightly colored nasturtiums. Gather large mature herb leaves that will cover a serving platter. Mince leaves and petals and sprinkle over vegetables.

Edible flowers. Perhaps you can't eat the daisies, but there are quite a few other blooms from the garden that have numerous culinary uses. When you gather flowers for eating, choose perfect, blemish-free specimens that have not been sprayed with any chemicals. Wash them quickly in cool water to remove dust and cut away the green stems to the base of the flower. Chill flowers in the refrigerator in a bowl of water or in a plasic bag to keep them fresh and crisp. Add them to dishes at the last minute. Use sparingly to create a special effect.

Choose whole flowers or mince petals to garnish canapes, toss in salads, float on drinks, sprinkle on soups, cook in eggs, finish off vegetable dishes, contrast with browned meats, and brighten desserts.

Among the flowers you can pick to eat are borage, calendulas, carnations and pinks, chives and onions, garland chrysanthemums, dandelions, fennel, geraniums, nasturtiums, rosemary, roses, burnet, and violets. Calendulas, like safflower petals, are good substitutes for saffron.

A tabletop herb garden. In parts of the Middle East it is customary to pass a bowl of fresh herb sprigs to eat along with the meal. For a pretty, edible bouquet, just collect whatever is available from your garden or market— parsley, watercress, chives, cress, dill, cilantro, green onions, tarragon, mint—and wash and chill. Arrange the sprigs in a bowl or basket. Include a few edible flowers such as borage, nasturtium, or violets, if in bloom. As a variation on the traditional idea, you could serve a spicy dip made from a yogurt base, or add the herbs to a light vinegar and oil dressing.

In Italy sprigs of fresh basil are served in little vases or vials of water on the table. Serving it in water keeps the herb from darkening or wilting.

Start your own tradition by placing a garden of herbs on the table. Give each guest a small pair of scissors along with their tableware and let them clip sprigs of fresh herbs to add to salads, soups, or other dishes.

Your tabletop garden may be just a pot of chives or several containers of assorted culinary plants. A couple of hours before dining wash the leaves under running water and allow to drain before putting the garden on the table. Arrange the potted herbs on a wicker tray, or large dish. You may wish to construct or purchase a wooden flat or shallow tray that holds small pots or nursery flats of herbs. With a slightly deeper tray you can plant a garden right inside to carry from window to table.

Remember fingerbowls? When you serve sticky finger-foods or messy shellfish, don't forget the old-fashioned fingerbowl. To a little bowl of warm water add a bit of lemon juice and leaves of scented geraniums, lemon verbena, mint, or other sweet herbs or flowers.

Using Preserved Herbs

To use dried herbs you need to break them up to release their stored flavor. You can simply pulverize them between your fingers as you add them to a dish or use a mortar and pestle to grind them as finely as you wish.

Since the essential oils become concentrated in the drying process, you will find that it usually takes less of the dried product in a recipe than it does of the fresh herb. The strength of the dried herb depends, however, on how it was harvested and preserved, how it has been stored, and how long you have had it on the shelf. The old rule of thumb is:

> ¼ teaspoon dried, finely powdered herb = ¾ to 1 teaspoon dried, loosely crumbled herb = 1½ to 2 teaspoons fresh chopped herb

Other equivalents to keep in mind are:

> ½ teaspoon garlic salt = 1 clove fresh garlic (increase or reduce other salt in recipe to compensate)
> 1 teaspoon dried dill seed = 1 head fresh dill
> 1 tablespoon dried onion flakes = 1 medium-size raw onion

When you use salt-cured herbs, remove the amount of leaves you will need and rinse away the salt just before adding them to a recipe.

To use frozen herbs, remove only the amount you will be using. Add the frozen herbs directly to foods to be cooked; let the herbs thaw before adding to cold foods. Once thawed, herbs that have been frozen cannot be refrozen.

If you have preserved herbs in vinegar, remove the desired amount, rinse, chop, and add to the recipe.

Combining herbs. Herbs are usually used in combination. When you blend your own, remember that strongly flavored herbs such as marjoram, rosemary, sage, and tarragon are best used alone or in combination with milder herbs whose flavors blend easily. In most instances avoid the conflict of two strongly flavored herbs that compete for attention.

The classic herb mix of French haute cuisine is known as *fines herbes*. This is a delicate combination of three or four herbs, preferably fresh, used to

Top: For a tabletop garden, construct a wooden box with inside dimensions the size of a standard nursery flat, a six-pack, or several small plastic pots. Seal the wood box with wood stain, or paint it.

Above: Drop the containers into place and enjoy an indoor herb garden. Before watering, remove the containers to a spot where they can drain well.

Use dried or fresh herbs in a *bouquet garni*.

flavor many dishes. The usual portions are equal parts parsley, chervil, chives, and tarragon. Other mild herbs may be substituted or added.

Bouquets garnis. Bouquet garni, or *fagot*, is a combination of several herbs, usually bay, thyme, and parsley or chervil simmered in dishes as they cook. Fresh herb sprigs are simply tied with string and dropped into the cooking pot. Leaves or dried herbs are wrapped inside a 4-inch square of cheese-cloth to form a bag and tied with string. You might also use a fine wire-mesh tea ball.

Here is a classic *bouquet garni* for soup, fish, or meat stocks:

Fresh bouquet garni

  2 sprigs thyme
  5 to 6 sprigs parsley
  1 bay leaf

Dried bouquet garni

  1 bay leaf
  1 tablespoon *each* crushed
     tarragon and parsley

  1 teaspoon *each* crushed
     rosemary and thyme

Many recipes call for a special *bouquet garni*, such as the spicy crab and shrimp boil that is unique to Louisiana. A favorite New Orleans combination follows:

Louisiana bouquet garni

  1 teaspoon *each* whole allspice,
     thyme, celery seed, and black
     peppercorns
  ½ teaspoon *each* cayenne and
     whole cloves

  5 bay leaves, broken
  3 dried hot chili peppers

Bring about 4 quarts of water to boil and add the seasoning bag along with salt to taste and sliced lemons. Boil for about 10 minutes before adding shellfish.

Mix your own blend. You may find it convenient to prepare in advance several premixed seasonings that you use often. This means you will not have to take the time to stir and blend each time you need something special.

Stuffing spices. All cooks know the value of herbs and spices to stuffings and dressings for pork, poultry, or veal. If you make stuffings often, try creating your own stuffing spice mix. Among the dried herbs that are excellent stuffing additions are sage, parsley, rosemary, marjoram, thyme, nutmeg, fennel, and oregano. Add other favorites and blend them to suit your taste buds.

Seasoned flour. Keep a jar of flour seasoned with herbs and spices to add to gravies and sauces, biscuits, or pizza crusts, or to dust foods before frying.

Simply add 1 to 2 teaspoons mixed dried herbs and spices to 2 cups flour. Add ½ teaspoon salt and freshly ground black pepper to taste. Seal tightly.

Spice Parisienne. Also known as *quatre épices*, this classic mixture of spices is used to enhance desserts and meats. Mix 1 tablespoon ground cinnamon with 1 teaspoon *each* ground cloves, ginger, and nutmeg.

Pickling spice. When pickling season approaches you might take the time to prepare a quantity of the pickling spices that are called for in many recipes. Prepare your own blend of herbs and spices by mixing various portions, according to taste, of whole allspice, bay leaves, black pepper-corns, cardamom, cinnamon sticks, cloves, coriander seed, dill seed, mus-tard seed, red peppers, ground ginger, and mace.

Chili powders. The commercial "spice" sold as chili powder is a mixture based on several types of sweet peppers (paprika) and hot peppers such as cayenne. Ingredients such as cumin, cloves, coriander, oregano, turmeric, black pepper, or garlic may be added. Pungency ranges from mild to fiery hot according to the amount of hot pepper used.

To blend your own chili seasoning, start with several tablespoons of paprika and add other spices according to taste. Mix small quantities to use as needed for Mexican and Spanish dishes or blend a larger portion of the spices together and store in an airtight jar. Use whenever you feel inspired to add a touch of chili flavor to eggs, rice, gravies, sauces, soups, fish, meats, and vegetables.

Curry powders. Curry seasonings are at their best when the spices are freshly ground and mixed together at the last minute. The busy cook, however, may want to blend enough favorite spices at one time to store in a tightly closed jar for instant spicing. Packaged in attractive jars or tins, curry powder is a good gift, too. Your own creation will undoubtedly be better suited to your way of cooking than commercial powders. Try this typical blend for starters.

4 tablespoons *each* seeds of coriander and fenugreek

1 teaspoon *each* seeds of mustard and fennel

2 tablespoons *each* cardamom seed, white peppercorns, and ground ginger

3 tablespoons ground turmeric

1 tablespoon cayenne or red chili (for hot curry) *or*
½ tablespoon pepper (for milder curry)

Grind ingredients together with a mortar and pestle, blender, or food processor.

Curry powders made at home are sure to be fresh—and the degree of their hotness can be controlled. In an attractive container, curry powders make spicy gifts.

Tangy Condiments

Herbs and spices are right at home when added to mustards, relishes, and salts. Try these suggestions as a starting point for your own creations.

Herb salt. A survey of the supermarket spice shelves will reveal a number of herb salts. You may prepare your own flavored salts for salad greens, fresh raw vegetables, and many cooked dishes. Reduce the amount of regular salt in the recipe when adding herb salt, or use in place of the suggested amount. Use only one kind of herb or blend combinations that please your taste. Dried lemon peel blends nicely with many herbs if you would like a salt that has a touch of lemon flavor.

Spread a thin layer of plain (noniodized) table salt on a baking sheet. Cover with a layer of fresh chopped herbs. Top with another layer of salt. Place in a medium oven (325°) for about 10 minutes. Break up lumps that result from leaf moisture and return to the oven for another 10 minutes or until leaves crumble easily.

Thoroughly blend the salt and herbs in a mortar and pestle or blender. Add ground pepper or paprika and dried ground spices, if desired. Store in tightly capped jars. Don't forget labels.

Making mustards. Everyone has a favorite taste in mustard and indeed there is great variety in flavors that can be created according to how you mix it. Once you have found the flavor you enjoy, you will never be happy with ready-made mustard again.

Making mustard is easy. It is best mixed in small quantities because although mustard keeps indefinitely, the flavor changes very rapidly.

To prepare hot mustard, use a cold liquid at the ratio of 2 or 3 tablespoons liquid to ¼ cup dry mustard powder.

For an English-style mustard, vinegar is the liquid. For a spicier taste, use white wine. For the French Dijon flavor, add champagne to the powder.

Flat beer turns mustard powder into the spicy Chinese variety. For the hottest of all, use plain water as the liquid.

To tone down the mustard, thin with a little milk, mayonnaise, or olive oil. The flavor of the mustard may be varied by adding sugar, pressed garlic, tarragon, or other spices to the powdered mustard before adding the liquid.

When the mustard is well blended, pour into a container and top with a lemon slice to help it retain freshness. Replace the lemon weekly. Seal with a tight-fitting cap and store in the refrigerator.

For a mild mustard enjoyed by many people on American hot dogs and burgers, try the following method: Place ½ cup dry mustard in a heat-proof dish. Add just enough boiling water to make a paste. Then cover the paste with boiling water to completely immerse it. Allow to stand for about 20 to 30 minutes, or until steaming stops. As it cools, churn the mustard away from the sides of the dish with a rubber spatula. Allow to settle for a few minutes and drain off the water.

Cover again with boiling water. Let stand for 5 minutes and drain again. Add 4 teaspoons sugar and 1 teaspoon salt or to taste. If you wish, add a little vinegar or other spices. For a bright yellow color, add 1 teaspoon turmeric. Pour into a container and allow to cool completely. Seal tightly and store at room temperature.

French herb mustard

¾ cup packed brown sugar
2 tablespoons flour
1½ tablespoons *each* dry
   mustard and mustard seed.
½ teaspoon turmeric
¼ teaspoon ground ginger

½ cup water
2 cups cider vinegar
½ teaspoon *each* dill seed,
   whole cloves and whole
   allspice

In a saucepan combine sugar, flour, mustard, mustard seed, turmeric and ginger. Stir in water and vinegar. Add the remaining spices tied in a cheesecloth bag or stainless steel tea infuser. Bring to boil, stirring. Simmer, covered, about 10 minutes or until slightly thickened. Store in covered jars in refrigerator.

Italian-style olives. In the Mediterranean manner, olives take on a new dimension when marinated with herbs, especially oregano. Offer them as an appetizer or as a relish with a meal.

1 can (15 oz.) jumbo pitted
   black olives, drained
2 teaspoons chopped fresh
   oregano *or* ½ teaspoon
   dried oregano

3 tablespoons olive oil
⅓ cup red wine vinegar
2 cloves garlic, minced
1 shallot, finely chopped

Place the olives in a jar or crock. Mix together the olive oil, vinegar, oregano, garlic, and shallot. Pour the mixture over the olives and mix well. Cover and chill for several days to allow the flavors to mellow. Makes 1 pint.

Nasturtium capers. If you do not grow real capers, you can make an acceptable substitute from the green buds of nasturtiums.

Cover the buds with a brine composed of 1 cup salt to 2 quarts water. Weight the buds down with a heavy plate to keep them immersed for 24 hours. Then remove the buds and soak them in cold water for 1 hour. Drain.

Bring distilled white vinegar to a boil. Pack the buds into sterilized jars to within ½ inch of the top and cover with the boiling vinegar. Seal and process in a boiling water bath for 10 minutes, or store in the refrigerator; use within a few weeks.

The long storage life of the horseradish lets you make small amounts at a time to ensure full piquance.

Coriander chutney. This fresh green chutney compliments Indian entrees: meatballs, curries, and kebabs. It is a relish that goes together in minutes with a blender.

1 cup fresh cilantro leaves
2 tablespoons shredded coconut
¼ teaspoon seasoned pepper
½ teaspoon *each* salt and sugar
3 tablespoons lemon juice
Dash liquid hot pepper seasoning

Place all the ingredients in a blender and blend just until pureed. Makes about ⅔ cup of sauce.

Horseradish. Fresh roots of horseradish will keep a long time when stored in a cool place. If you do not grow your own, stock up from the produce markets when the fresh roots are available, usually in late summer and early fall. Horseradish roots also freeze successfully. Like dried horseradish, after about 3 months the roots become bitter.

To assure full potency make small batches of horseradish frequently and do not store it more than 2 or 3 weeks.

Peel the washed roots, grate or cube the desired amount, and put through a food processor or blender with vinegar, salt, and sugar to taste. Pack in jars, cap tightly, and store in the refrigerator.

If you must resort to dried horseradish root powder, reconstitute it about 30 minutes before serving. Mix 1 tablespoon dried powder in 2 tablespoons water and add about ½ cup heavy cream. Just before serving add salt, sugar, and a bit of vinegar to taste.

Serve fresh or reconstituted horseradish with cold meats, smoked fish, sausages, and frankfurters. Stir into seafood cocktail sauces, potato or pasta salads, as well as French dressings. Blend with whipped cream for a quick cold buffet sauce. Add to hot cream or white sauces and serve with boiled or corned beef, London broil, or prime rib.

Herb-pickled beets. This quick recipe produces a tangy side-dish that is as visually appealing as it is tasty.

6 medium-size cooked beets, sliced
2 sweet onions, thinly sliced
1 teaspoon fresh marjoram, minced
1 clove garlic, crushed
Pinch nutmeg, freshly grated
Salt and pepper to taste
2 tablespoons sugar
4 tablespoons olive oil
4 tablespoons wine vinegar

Mix beets, onions, marjoram, garlic, nutmeg, salt, and pepper well. Mix sugar, oil, and vinegar separately and pour over beet mixture. Let stand for an hour, cover, and chill.

Well-Dressed Salads

Certainly one of the greatest rewards of an herb garden is harvesting fresh ingredients for salads and salad dressings.

Herb dressing. Use basil, dill, marjoram, oregano, sage, tarragon, thyme, or other culinary favorites in this reliable oil and vinegar dressing.

6 tablespoons oil
3 tablespoons vinegar
¼ teaspoon *each* salt and dry mustard
Freshly ground pepper to taste
1 to 2 cloves garlic, peeled and minced or pressed
2 to 3 tablespoons fresh herbs, minced, *or* 1 tablespoon dried herbs, crushed

Combine and shake well.

For fruit salads omit the mustard and garlic and add sugar or honey to taste. Use poppyseed, rosemary, tarragon, or other sweet herbs.

Tarragon, garlic, shallot, sage, fresh green peppercorns, and oregano are among the many herbs that can be used to flavor vinegar.

Flavored vinegars. Some of the most pleasurable concoctions you can make with herbs and spices are flavored vinegars. Colorful and varied vinegars in interesting bottles are not only visual assets to the kitchen shelves, but also convenient when you want to perk up a salad dressing or add zest to dishes calling for vinegar.

You can use almost every herb and spice, alone or in combination. Experiment with small quantities of various mixes to find flavors you enjoy. Attractive bottles with a sprig of an herb immersed in the vinegar make welcome gifts: Take a corked bottle of flavored vinegar instead of wine to your next dinner party; your hosts will be delighted.

The flavoring procedure is simple. Add 4 ounces fresh herb or spice, or 2 ounces of the dried version, to each quart of cold vinegar. Leave for 5 to 6 weeks to develop flavor. Then strain the vinegar into clean bottles, or leave fresh herb twigs in for show. Cap tightly and store. (You can seal with hot wax to which pungent powdered cinnamon has been added.) Your palate will let you know if you need to add more or less of the herb or spice next time you make another batch.

As the base you can use any of several store-bought vinegars—white, wine, cider, or malt. White vinegar will let the flavor of the herb or spice predominate. Other vinegars add their own characteristics to the end product.

If you want flavored vinegar in a hurry, bring the vinegar and spices to a boil and simmer for about 20 minutes. Pour into bottles and cap. It is ready to use without waiting for it to mellow.

Tabbouli salad. This refreshing and unusual salad from the Middle East uses garden-fresh herbs as its main ingredients. You may wish to add diced green peppers or avocados.

1 cup bulgur (cracked wheat)	Freshly grated black pepper, to taste
2 cups boiling water	1 teaspoon allspice
2 cups parsley, finely chopped	½ cup olive oil
½ cup green onions, finely chopped	3 ripe tomatoes, peeled and diced
½ cup fresh mint, chopped, *or* ¼ cup dried mint, crumbled	Lettuce leaves, preferably romaine
½ cup lemon juice	Lemon wedges
½ teaspoon salt, or to taste	

Pour boiling water over the bulgur in a bowl and let stand 1 hour. Drain and return to bowl. Add the parsley, onions, mint, lemon juice, salt, pepper, and allspice. Blend well and chill.

Just before serving toss with oil and chopped tomatoes. Serve on lettuce and garnish with lemon.

Green goddess dressing. Chives play a part in this famous San Francisco dressing—a perfect party dip as well as a flavorful dressing for chicken and seafood salads.

2 egg yolks	¾ cup safflower or other vegetable oil
1 tablespoon lemon juice	½ cup finely chopped parsley
4 tablespoons tarragon-flavored white wine vinegar	2 tablespoons finely cut chives
2 teaspoons Dijon-style mustard	2 shallots, peeled
1 teaspoon salt	4 anchovy fillets (optional)
	⅓ cup sour cream

In a blender place egg yolks, lemon juice, vinegar, mustard, and salt. Blend a few seconds. With motor running, gradually pour in the oil in a slow steady stream. Add parsley, chives, shallots, and anchovies and blend a few seconds. Stir in sour cream, and turn into a sauce bowl. Chill. Makes about 2 cups.

To serve as a dip, use with raw vegetables such as chilled raw radishes, whole 1-inch mushrooms, diagonally cut carrot and celery slices, turnip wedges, green pepper strips, cucumber slices, and whole cherry tomatoes with stems.

Butters, Cheeses, and Sauces

The following ideas blend garden-fresh or dried seasonings in spreads, dips, or smooth sauces. Experiment with variations.

Herb butters. Flavored butter adds a special touch to hot breads, baked potatoes, and vegetables. It's a tasty sandwich spread and makes an event of a stack of toast. Use it to cook eggs or toss noddles and other pasta. Melt it on broiled meats and fish.

Any of your favorite herbs will make delicious butter. Use 1 tablespoon fresh minced herb or 1 teaspoon dried herb or crushed seed to each ¼ cup softened butter, sweet or salted as you prefer. Mix well and pack into small dishes or form into butter balls. Refrigerate overnight to fully develop the flavor.

A special treat for guests would be a variety of herb butters at the table. Identify each flavor with a garnish of the fresh herb.

Herb cheese and mayonnaise. Transform cottage cheese or cream cheese into dips and spreads by adding herbs and spices. To 8 ounces of softened cream cheese, or ½ pound of cottage cheese, add 2 tablespoons minced fresh herbs or 1 teaspoon dried herbs or spices. Combine compatible flavors

Fresh or dried herbs turn cottage cheese, cream cheese, sour cream, or mayonnaise into delicious dips. Spice them with homemade curry powder.

as desired. Add a bit of pepper sauce if you like it hot. If you want a smoother or thinner product add sour cream, yogurt, or mayonnaise. Make several hours or a day ahead of serving and leave in the refrigerator to develop the flavors.

A well-seasoned cheeseball is appreciated at a party or as a gift. Start with feta cheese or a good, sharp grated cheddar. Combine with butter, herbs, and spices according to taste. Form into balls with your hands. For a festive touch, roll the cheese balls in finely chopped nuts, finely minced fresh herbs, or crushed seeds. Wrap in cheesecloth, foil, or waxed paper and refrigerate for at least a full day. Bring to room temperature about an hour before serving. Garnish with fresh herbs.

Seasoned mayonnaise can serve as a dip for raw vegetables, a sandwich spread, or a dressing for cold seafood or mixed vegetable salads.

Make your favorite mayonnaise or use a commercial product. Stir in minced fresh herbs, a bit of lemon peel, and whatever spices you enjoy. Mix well; chill.

Körözött liptói. This delectable party dip is a variation on a cheese spread from Liptó in northern Hungary where liptauer cheese—a sheep's milk cheese—originates.

1 cup cottage cheese, sieved	1 tablespoon caraway seeds
1 cup butter or margarine, softened	1 tablespoon dry mustard
	1 chopped anchovy (optional)
1 tablespoon *each* minced capers and chives	Paprika

Combine all ingredients and beat smooth. Dust with paprika. Makes 2 cups.

Fresh basil leaves are the secret of pesto sauce, an Italian classic, served over pasta.

Pesto sauce. One of the great Italian contributions to the world of food is this sauce made from fresh basil. It is usually served on pasta cooked *al dente*. Try a bit also in vegetable soups, on baked potatoes, broiled fish, or golden spaghetti squash.

2	cups firmly packed fresh basil leaves, washed and drained	3	cloves garlic, peeled
¼	cup pignoli (pine nuts), walnuts, or pistachios	¾	cup freshly grated Parmesan cheese
		½	cup olive oil

Blend basil, nuts, and garlic until pureed. Blend in cheese. Slowly add oil while blending on low speed. Serve immediately or add a thin layer of olive oil, cover and refrigerate. The oil keeps the sauce from darkening until serving time.

While basil is in season make plenty of pesto and freeze small quantities of it in individual containers or plastic bags. Thaw at room temperature for 2 hours before serving or place in a bowl of hot water for about 20 minutes before opening.

Do not attempt pesto with dried basil. You can use fresh parsley for a tasty difference.

Herb pasta. In lieu of pesto, this is another easy sauce that's delicious on hot spaghetti or other pasta.

Mince ½ cup fresh herbs such as chives, basil, parsley, thyme, savory, oregano, or whatever is in the garden. Mix the herbs with ½ cup softened butter. Quickly sauté several cloves of crushed garlic in ½ cup olive oil and add the butter mixture to melt. Pour over pasta and toss. Add freshly grated Romano or Parmesan cheese to individual taste.

Basting sauce and marinade for meats. To impart the flavors of herbs and spices, marinate meats prior to cooking or baste with herb sauce as they cook. Suggested seasonings:

☐ Beef. Bay, oregano, rosemary, savory, thyme.
☐ Lamb. Basil, coriander, cumin, mint, parsely, rosemary.
☐ Pork. Anise, caraway, cumin, nutmeg, parsley, rosemary, thyme.
☐ Poultry. Basil, parsley, rosemary, tarragon.

For basting. To each cup of meat stock, add ½ cup wine and 2 tablespoons fresh herbs or 1 tablespoon dried. Simmer together for 10 minutes. Baste meat several times.

For marinade. Combine 1 cup oil, ½ cup wine or vinegar, salt and pepper to taste, 1 clove crushed garlic, and herbs and spices to taste. Pour over meat, cover, and refrigerate. Let stand, turning meat a couple of times an hour so all portions are marinated.

Add New Flavors to Baking

The wonderful aroma of herbed bread baking in the oven is an added delight to its flavorful taste.

To a basic bread or biscuit dough add 2 tablespoons of minced, fresh chives, dill, marjoram, sage, savory, or thyme, or use 2 teaspoons of any of these herbs dried. Try mixing several herbs and ground spices.

Seeds of caraway, dill, fennel, anise, sesame, and the familiar poppy make

Herbs and spices blended into bread dough or seeds sprinkled over the top of a loaf enhance the already irresistible aroma of homebaked bread—and add to the flavor and appearance too.

interesting and tasty toppings on breads, rolls, biscuits, and cookies. Just brush the dough with egg yolk and sprinkle with seeds before baking.

Seeds can be used in less familiar ways. Add fennel to apple and berry pies, cobblers, or tarts. Crushed coriander gives a new dimension to hot gingerbread. To vary a basic cookie dough or cake batter, add crushed coriander, anise, dill, sesame, or fennel before baking. Stir in a few toasted sesame seeds next time you make a pie crust. Create a new dessert by substituting toasted sesame seeds for the pecans in your favorite pecan pie recipe. Also add a half cup of raisins for a flavor contrast.

Herb pastry mix for quiche. For each 9-inch pastry shell combine 1½ cups flour, 1 tablespoon dried parsley flakes, 2 teaspoons dill weed, 1½ teaspoons dry mustard, and ½ teaspoon salt. You can mix enough for several crusts and store in a tightly covered jar.

When you are ready for a crust, cut ½ cup butter or margarine into 1½ cups of the pastry mix until it resembles coarse meal. Sprinkle in 4 to 5 tablespoons cold water, a tablespoon at a time, until the mix is moist enough to leave sides of bowl. Gather into a ball and roll out on floured surface to ⅛-inch thick. Line quiche pan or pie plate. Prick with a fork, brush with beaten egg and bake at 400°F (204°C) for 10 minutes. Prepare any quiche filling, pour it into the partially baked shell, and finish the baking according to your recipe.

Herb cheddar loaf. A trio of herbs—marjoram, oregano, and thyme—mingle in this cheese-streaked round of fragrant bread. The loaf is at its best served hot from the oven, or you should plan to reheat it in foil. It makes a fine luncheon bread served with sliced tomatoes and red onions, along with assorted cold meats or meat loaf.

1 package active dry yeast	1 teaspoon *each* dried
¼ cup warm water	oregano, marjoram, and
½ cup milk	thyme
⅓ cup butter	3¼ cups all-purpose flour
1 tablespoon sugar	1½ cups shredded cheddar
½ teaspoon salt	cheese
3 eggs	1 egg white

Sprinkle yeast into warm water and let stand until dissolved. Heat milk and butter until butter melts; pour into a mixing bowl. Add sugar and salt and let cool to lukewarm. Add eggs, one at a time, and beat until smooth. Mix in the yeast mixture and herbs. Gradually add 2 cups of the flour and beat until smooth. Add remaining flour and cheese and beat with a heavy-duty electric mixer or wooden spoon. Turn out on a lightly floured board and knead until smooth and satiny. Place in a bowl, cover with a damp towel, and let rise in a warm place until doubled in size.

Turn out dough on a board and knead lightly. Place in a greased 2-quart round casserole or soufflé dish. Cover and let rise until doubled in bulk. Brush the top with lightly beaten egg white. Bake in a 350° oven for 35 minutes, or until the loaf sounds hollow when thumped. Place on a rack and let cool slightly. Turn out of dish. Makes 1 large loaf.

Sugar and Spice

Edible parts of herbs and spices can be turned into treats to satisfy the sweet tooth.

Crystallized leaves and petals. Sugar-coated herb petals and leaves can be used as garnishes for desserts or eaten as candy. Pick roses, violets, johnny-jump-ups, or attractive leaves of borage, sage, mint, or other sweet foliage.

Wash the petals or leaves quickly and gently pat dry with a paper towel. Remove individual petals. Cut away the bitter white tip of rose petals.

Marjoram, oregano, and thyme from the herb garden flavor a round herb cheddar loaf.

Beat egg whites until foamy and brush on each side of the leaves or petals with a pastry brush or your fingers. Surfaces should be moist but with no excess egg white.

Shake or dust fine granulated white sugar on both sides. Place gently on a tray. Dry in the refrigerator for several days.

Candied blossoms. Violets, borage, roses, geraniums, violas, and other edible flowers are graceful finishing touches on custards, cakes, ice creams, sherbets, parfaits, and other light desserts. Or simply serve them in a bowl or little basket as candy.

Start with about 3 cups of flowers. Wash quickly and remove stems. Pat dry with paper towels.

Combine 3 cups white sugar with 2 cups water, bring to boil and cook to the soft crack stage—about 238°F (114°C) on a candy thermometer. Pour about half the syrup into a shallow pan and let both quantities cool. Position the flowers on a rack inside the pan so they float on the syrup. Cover the top of the pan with a damp cloth and let it sit in a cool place for several hours. Then cover the flowers with the remaining cooled syrup. Let stand at least 12 hours in a cool place with a cloth over the pan to keep dust out.

Remove the rack and place it where the flowers can drain and dry. When completely dried, store flowers in an airtight container between layers of waxed paper to prevent them from sticking together.

Candied angelica or lovage stems. The stalks of angelica and lovage can be candied and used as a fruitcake ingredient or garnish.

Harvest mature stalks and cut into pieces 3 or 4 inches long. Soak 12 hours in a solution of cold water and 1 tablespoon *each* of salt and vinegar. Drain and cover with fresh water. Boil until stalks are transparent.

Make a syrup of 2 cups white sugar and 1 cup water. Add a few drops of green food coloring, if desired. Place the stems in the syrup and simmer until transparent and glazed. Place on a tray until dry. Store in airtight containers in a cool place.

Horehound candy. A generation ago this bittersweet candy was made as a cough suppressant.

Boil 1 quart chopped horehound leaves and stems in a pint of water for 30 minutes to make a strong decoction. Strain and reserve liquid. To the liquid add 3 cups white sugar and bring to a boil. Add ¼ cup butter and continue cooking until the syrup will form a hard ball in cold water—300°F (121°C) on a candy thermometer. Pour into a buttered shallow pan and score into pieces before it sets. When candy has cooled and is hard, break into pieces and wrap individually in waxed paper. Store in a closed container.

Spiced sugar. To flavor granulated sugar, consider using leaves of scented geraniums, mints, sweet cicely, lemon balm, or petals of roses, pinks, or violets. For spiced sugar add ground cinnamon, cloves, ginger, or allspice. Store on your spice shelf and add to puddings, toppings, meringues, syrups, cereals, waffles, crepes, or beverages.

Put alternating layers of granulated white or brown sugar and leaves, petals, or spices in a widemouthed crock or other container. Close tightly. After a couple of weeks mix thoroughly. Store in airtight containers.

Herbal honey. Fill a jar with any honey you prefer. Add a whole bay leaf, or several pieces of crystallized ginger studded with whole cloves—or several thin slices of lemon and a cinnamon stick.

Herb or spice jellies. Jellies made from apple or other fruit juices and herbs or spices are good with roast meats; they also make tasty gifts. You may adapt the basic recipe to almost any culinary herb: basil, fennel, mint, rosemary, sage, scented geraniums, thyme. Suitable spices include allspice, cloves, cinnamon, and ginger.

Add a delicate flavor to honey with herbs and spices.

3 cups fruit juice
¼ to ½ cup fresh herb, chopped, *or* 2 tablespoons dried herb *or* spice seed, crushed
2 tablespoons cider vinegar
3 to 3½ cups granulated sugar
½ cup liquid pectin
Fresh herb sprigs or whole spices (optional)
Few drops food coloring (optional)

Bring 1 cup of the fruit juice to a rolling boil, pour over herb or spice and let stand 20 minutes. Strain into large saucepan. Add vinegar, the remaining 2 cups of fruit juice, and appropriate coloring, if desired. Mix in sugar and bring to a boil. Stir in pectin and boil 1 minute more. Remove from heat and skim off foam. Pour into hot, sterilized pint or half-pint jars. Add a sprig or few leaves of the herb or pieces of the spice on top or immerse in the jelly. Use melted paraffin wax or lids to seal.

Some fruit juice and herb combinations are:

☐ Cloves and tangerine juice
☐ Mint and apple juice
☐ Marjoram and orange juice
☐ Tarragon and grape juice
☐ Thyme and crabapple juice

Rose hip jam and jelly. Few foods from the garden rival the fruit of roses for concentrated food value. It is one of the richest sources of vitamin C and contains large amounts of other vitamins and minerals. Old species of roses, especially *Rosa rugosa*, produce the tastiest and most nutritious hips. Use only those that have not been sprayed with chemicals. Harvest when the hips turn bright orange-red. Remove blossom ends and stems and wash well. Both the jam and the jelly can be made from dried rose hips available in health-food stores.

Spice up homemade jelly or add an herbal essence to a delicate fruit flavor.

To make jam: Simmer 2 cups of rose hips in 2 cups of water until tender, mashing the fruit while it cooks to release juices. Push the fruit through a fine sieve. Add 1 cup sugar for each cup pulp. Cook until the mixture has the consistency of jam. Pour into sterilized jars and seal with melted paraffin wax or lids.

For jelly: Soak 1 quart dried apples overnight in enough water to cover. The following morning clean 1 quart of rose hips and combine with the apples in a pan with just enough water to cover. Cook until tender. Drain through a jelly bag. Add 2 cups sugar to each pint of juice and boil about 20 minutes, or until the mixture jells into a thick mass when dropped from a spoon into cold water. Pour into sterilized jars and seal.

Rose petal jam. Make this jam for an exotic taste treat on muffins, cakes, and toast. Use sparingly until you develop a taste for rose flavor; a little goes a long way. You need:

    1 pound fresh rose petals
    2 pounds sugar

Pack layers of petals tightly in a large crock with alternating layers of sugar, finishing with a layer of sugar. Cover with hot water. Put a damp cloth over the crock and let stand for 3 days.

Prepare a syrup, using enough water to dissolve one pound of sugar. Cook the syrup to soft-ball stage, 234° to 240°F (112° to 116°C), then add the rose petals and any juice they formed. Let the mixture simmer until it reaches the consistency of honey. Remove from heat and stir in lemon juice. Pour into hot sterilized jars and seal.

Herbal and Spice Teas

Classically, tea refers to the leaves of the oriental shrub *Camellia sinensis* (formerly called *Thea sinensis*). The term "tea" has come to apply to all drinks made from steeping leaves, flowers, seeds, roots, or bark in hot water. In the broad sense all teas are "herbal" teas since they are made from useful plant parts. Current usage, however, classifies oriental teas separately from non-caffeine herbal teas.

Oriental tea comes in three forms: black (fermented), Oolong (semifermented) from India, and Ceylon and green (unfermented) from China and Japan. Prices vary according to variety and quality.

To brew a perfect pot of tea start with a good quality loose tea. Warm a nonmetal teapot with hot water and drain. Put 1 teaspoon of tea in the pot for each cup, plus an extra one for the pot. Bring freshly drawn water to a boil and immediately pour over the leaves. Steep 3 to 5 minutes, stirring the leaves once to distribute flavor. Pour through a strainer into teacups or glasses. You may add a sweetener, lemon, or milk as you prefer.

If the tea proves too strong, add hot water. A proper tea table always has a pot of hot water handy. If you are making tea to serve over ice, add extra leaves for a stronger brew to allow for the melting ice.

For variety, mix into any tea a few dried or fresh herb leaves, bits of lemon or orange peel, flowers, pieces of cinnamon or vanilla bean, cloves, or other whole spices. Store tea leaves or mixes in tight containers, preferably tin boxes.

Even though herbal teas are growing in popularity in America, they are certainly not new. They have been enjoyed in many countries for centuries. Herbal drinks were known in Europe long before oriental teas were introduced. American Indians and colonists drank herbal concoctions. The Orientals wonder why we import so much of their tea when we have sage in our gardens; New Englanders have enjoyed sage tea sweetened with a bit of maple syrup for generations. From South America comes *yerba maté* made from a member of the holly family. The rest of the world is now discovering the delicious flavor of *maté*, which contains a small amount of caffeine.

Another caffeine tea can be brewed from the African cola nut which is used in cola drinks.

Herbal teas may be made from just one kind of herb or a mixture of several, with flowers and spices added if you like. Elaborate blends are available commercially, but try experimenting and pack your own favorite blends in tins for gift giving or to enjoy yourself.

Teas brewed from the leaves of herbs are also called tisanes. Most are made by *infusion*, that is, by steeping in hot water. Start with 2 to 3 teaspoons of fresh or frozen leaves or 1 to 2 teaspoons of dried herb per cup in a nonmetal teapot that has been warmed. Cover with boiling water and steep 5 to 10 minutes. Strain into cups.

Sweeteners or lemon may be added as desired. Milk is rarely used with herbal teas as it clouds the drink and disguises the subtle flavors. All herbal

Teas from the Orient may be black, Oolong, or green. But Oriental exporters wonder why Americans overlook the wealth of tea herbs in their own backyards.

teas may be served iced. Just make them a little stronger to allow for the melting ice.

Some herb leaves, as well as seeds, roots, and bark must be prepared by *decoction*—boiling the herb in water to draw out the flavors. Add the herb or spice to water at about the same ratio as in steeped tea. Boil for 15 to 20 minutes and strain into teacups. Add lemon or sweeteners as desired.

The accompanying table shows methods of brewing for a variety of herbal and spice teas.

Herbal teas from leaves
Made by infusion, steeping in hot water.

Alfalfa	Germander	Oat straw
Angelica	Great mullein	Red clover
Blackberry	Horehound	Rosemary
Borage	Lemongrass	Sage
Catnip	Lemon verbena	Savory
Coltsfoot	Malua	Scented geraniums
Comfrey	Marjoram	Strawberry
Damiana	Maté	Thyme
Dill	Mint	Wood betony
Dittany of Crete		

Made by decoction, boiling in water.

Agrimony	Bergamot	Lemon balm

Herbal teas from flowers
Made by infusion.

Calendula	Hibiscus	Malva
Chamomile	Jasmine	Rose
Goldenrod	Lime	

Herbal teas from seeds, roots, and bark
Made by decoction or boiling.

Anise	Chicory	Ginger
Asparagus	Cinnamon	Ginseng
Birch	Dandelion	Sassafras
Cardamom		

The following is a decoction made from fresh ginger root that deserves special attention. It provides perfect refreshment on a cold day and is delicious iced.

Scott's ginger tea. Grate or chop about 2 tablespoons fresh ginger root (no need to peel) into 4 cups water. Add half a lemon, sliced. Bring to a boil and continue boiling, uncovered, for about 15 to 20 minutes. Strain into cups. Add honey to taste. For variety, add a cinnamon stick, a few cardamom seeds, or whole cloves along with fresh ginger.

Coffee and Its Substitutes

We can think of coffee as an herbal drink since it is made from the seed of *Coffea arabica*. Buy the beans, roasted or green, whole or ground, and store in the refrigerator (if ground) or freezer (if whole bean) to maintain its freshness longer. If you roast your own you can control the richness of the brew. Grinding the roasted beans just before brewing insures a better taste.

There are numerous coffee makers on the market. Make coffee according to directions that come with your pot or brewing equipment. Most coffee lovers prefer the flavor made from dripping methods over those that perk or boil the brew.

To add an occasional spicy touch to dessert coffee, add a whole cardamom seed or a few crushed coriander seeds to the cup. Since cinnamon and coffee are good companions, add a sprinkle before making the coffee or use a cinnamon stick to stir the brew. Top with whipped cream and sprinkle with cinnamon.

Many people cannot or prefer not to drink coffee which is high in caffeine. They can substitute decaffeinated beans or other herbs. New Orleans has made the addition of chicory root to coffee famous, but chicory can also be brewed alone as a coffee replacement. Other people enjoy asparagus seeds, dandelion root, English oak acorns, hawthorn seeds, kava-kava, milk thistle seeds, soybeans, or witch grass roots. All these substitutes are roasted and ground.

Other Beverages

On a cold evening a welcome treat is hot mulled cider, wine, or apple juice. Pour the chosen beverage into a saucepan. Combine such spices as cinnamon sticks, whole cloves, allspice, citrus peel, or flower petals in a cheesecloth bag or wire mesh tea ball. Simmer for about 15 minutes or longer, but do not boil. Pour and garnish with spices.

Freshly ground nutmeg is delicious in hot steamed milk (with a piece of vanilla bean), cold eggnog, or other milk-based beverages.

For tasty cold punches, start with a base of iced herbal tea, add whatever fruit juices you like along with sparkling wine, carbonated ginger ale, or soda water. Blend together. Add a ring or block of ice in which you have frozen sprigs of herbs or flowers. Garnish the bowl, pitcher, or glasses with borage leaves and flowers, any of the mints, rose petals, or violets.

Dandelion wine. Pick dandelion flowers that have just begun to open. Harvest only those you know have not been sprayed with any chemical. Follow this old New England recipe.

2½ gallons dandelion flowers, removed from stems	10 pounds sugar
	4 gallons lukewarm water
6 oranges, thinly sliced	

Make 6 alternate layers of flowers, sugar, and oranges in a 5-gallon crock. Pour water over and cover with a cloth. Leave at room temperature until bubbling stops, usually about 3 weeks. Strain the sweet wine into bottles through a double layer of cheesecloth. Cap bottles and store in cool dry place.

Dried petals and fragrant leaves capture the
memory of a summer garden in potpourris
and pretty fabric sachets.

CREATIVE USES FOR HERBS AND SPICES

Use herbs and spices to scent, soothe, and decorate. Light a fragrant candle, rest on an herbal pillow, hang a bay leaf wreath.

The fragrance, color, and beauty of the plant forms of herbs and spices assures their use in many different forms and preparations. The long tradition of their use and the sentiments and symbols ascribed to them give a romantic and meaningful dimension to homemade crafts and gifts.

Preserving Garden Fragrances

The fragrances of a garden bring back memories to each of us. A certain smell can take you back to some special place, time, or event, even if you are not consciously aware of the association. As Rudyard Kipling noted, "Scents are surer than sounds or sights to make your heart strings crack." The heady, nostalgic aromas that blend together so perfectly in the garden can be captured in potpourris and other concoctions that last indefinitely.

Even if you do not garden, it is possible to buy dried petals, leaves, spices, and oils, the same ingredients that are the basis of costly perfumes, to create your own special scents at home. Herb and spice shops, as well as health-food stores and soap shops, offer many kinds of dried leaves and petals and essential oils. Other ingredients are available at pharmacies.

Potpourris, Sachets, and Tussie Mussies

Long before modern air fresheners came in cans, the leaves, flowers, seeds, roots, and barks of herbs and spices were carried in hand bouquets, strewn on the floor, or preserved in special blends to freshen the air or mask unwanted odors.

A floral or spicy potpourri can perfume a room or be stuffed into tiny pillows for freshening clothes or linen. Or you can stuff a larger pillow for pleasant afternoon napping.

Potpourris are blends of flowers, fragrant leaves, and spices with a fixative added to preserve the essential oils. Orrisroot, sweet flag, benzoin, storax, and ambergris are the most commonly used fixatives. It is easy to grow your own orrisroot or sweet flag but all these fixatives are available at drugstores or from herbalists. A few drops of fragrant oils complete the mixes.

Moist potpourri. Potpourris in earlier times were made by the moist method where herbs are salted down in a crock, then mixed with spices, oils, a fixative, and a bit of brandy or good perfume. The fragrances last for many years.

To make the old-fashioned moist version, start with petals and fragrant leaves collected from the garden. Dry them only partially, for just a few days, until they are limp but not crisp. Layer the petals with noniodized salt in a widemouthed container, adding spices, a fixative, fragrant oils, and brandy or alcohol-based perfume. Place a weight on top of the mixture to help draw out the oils. Cover tightly.

Open the container, remove the weight and stir the mixture every day for

Leave the lid to a potpourri box on tight until you want to release the sweet fragrance.

about a month or until the fragrances have blended and mellowed. Then pour the mixture into a large bowl and mix very thoroughly. Pack into small containers of opaque glass, porcelain, or silver that have removable lids. Open the cover whenever you wish to enjoy the fragrance. If the potpourri seems to be drying out, add a little perfume or good brandy over the top and stir to activate the oils.

Half-century potpourri. The following is one recipe for moist potpourri that you can use as a guide for creating your own. It is called the half-century potpourri because the fragrance lasts 50 years or more.

¾ cup salt (noniodized)
3 bay leaves, crushed
¼ cup allspice, crushed
¼ cup cloves, crushed
¼ cup brown sugar
1 tablespoon orrisroot powder
1 quart partially dried rose petals, preferably old species roses

2 cups mixed, partially dried, fragrant garden flowers (such as jasmine, lavender, orange blooms, violets)
1 cup dried fragrant leaves (such as rose geranium, lemon balm, lemon verbena)
2 tablespoons brandy

Mix together the salt, bay, allspice, cloves, and sugar. Blend flower petals and leaves with the orrisroot. Place some of the petal mixture in a large crock and sprinkle with the salt mixture. Continue alternating layers of petals and salt, ending with salt. Add the brandy, weight down with a plate, and cap tightly. After stirring every day and mixing thoroughly at the end of a month, pour into small containers.

This old recipe will keep its fragrance for up to 50 years with the addition of a bit of brandy every few years or whenever the mixture dries out.

Dry potpourri. Dry potpourri begins with thoroughly dried, crisp petals and leaves. Then they are combined with fixatives, spices, and fragrant oils, stored in a covered container for several weeks, and shaken from time to time to blend. After the mellowing period, place in small containers with removable lids or stuff into little bags or pillows as sachets. A typical dry potpourri goes like this:

San Francisco potpourri

1 quart dried flower petals
1 cup small whole flowers (dried in silica gel or borax)
2 cups dried fragrant leaves
1 tablespoon crushed orrisroot
2 tablespoons dried citrus peel
1 tablespoon *each* whole cloves, allspice, cardamom seed; all crushed

1 teaspoon anise seed, crushed
1 whole nutmeg, crushed
2 bay leaves, broken
4 cinnamon sticks, broken
1 vanilla bean, broken
Several drops *each* oils of patchouli, jasmine, rose geranium, lilac, and tuberose

Place petals, blooms and leaves in a large container that has a tight-fitting lid, packing loosely so there is plenty of room to shake the mixture. Sprinkle with orrisroot. Add the citrus peel and spices and mix together gently. Sprinkle the oils on top and close tightly. Shake the container every few days for about six weeks or until the mixture is well mellowed. Then pack into smaller containers, sachets, or gift packages.

It is difficult to predict the exact fragrance you will end up with when you make potpourri. Much depends upon the condition, variety, and freshness of the flowers and foliages you start with as well as how they are dried. Refer to our list of fragrant garden plants (page 51) for suggested herbs to include in potpourri. Take a walk through your garden and look for any flowers and leaves that smell good. Also collect a few flowers that have nice color even if they do not have a fragrance. They will add to the visual quality of a dry potpourri.

Far left: Tiny herbal pillow sachets scent linens or clothing.

Left: Make your own sachets from fabric that reflects what's inside.

Collect ingredients for potpourri all through the gardening season, harvesting when flowers and leaves are at their peak. Dry them according to the methods outlined on pages 29–30. Store each type of foliage or bloom in separate plastic bags until you are ready to blend them. Be sure that all leaves and flowers are completely dry before you start mixing them since a few moldy petals or leaves can spoil the whole batch.

When you make dry potpourri that will be displayed, add some small whole blooms dried by one of the desiccants (see page 31) for bright touches of color. Collect and dry berries, cones, or other decorative materials from the garden to add interest to the mixture.

Dry potpourri is most attractive stored in clear glass where you can see the ingredients. But you can use any container for display. A cover keeps the mixture fresh much longer. Just remove it when you want to release the scent. If you prefer, you can store the finished products in plastic bags or jars and pour out a little into bowls or baskets to add fragrance to the air. The scent will last a few weeks or perhaps as long as 1 or 2 months when constantly exposed to the air.

Sachets. Sachets are little bags or envelopes filled with dried potpourri. Traditionally, they are added to clothes drawers, linen closets, sweater boxes, or anywhere you want a fresh clean scent.

To make old-fashioned sachets, wrap potpourri inside pretty handkerchiefs or squares of very thin fabric and tie into little balls or fold into interesting shapes. Finish off with bits of lace and ribbons or maybe a dried flower.

If you want sachets that lie flat, make bags or envelopes first, crush the potpourri into a fine powder and fill the little envelope. Stitch closed and add lace, ribbons, appliqué, or other decorative touches. With a little imagination you can create beautiful sachets to keep or give.

If you would like sachets that repel moths, stuff with southernwood, wormwood, thyme, lavender, santolina, or tansy. Lay or tie the bags around winter garments in storage.

If you want a pillow, make a large envelope of a soft fabric and stuff part of it, a quilted section, or an appliqué with the potpourri. If you have lots of herbs, stuff the whole pillow. Herbal pillows are thoughtful gifts for persons confined to bed. What could be more pleasant than resting your head on a scented pillow that transports you to the garden?

When you make sachets don't forget the cats. Dried catnip leaves can be stuffed into little fabric mice or other fantasy creatures to bring hours of delight to your own pets or those of friends.

Tussie mussies. The Elizabethans carried little nosegays of fresh herbs and flowers known as tussie mussies to overpower objectionable odors. It

Above: The herbal-floral nosegay known as the tussie mussie dates from Elizabethan times.

Opposite: Clove-studded citrus pomanders give off their spicy scent for years. Eucalyptus pods also retain their sweet pungence for a long time.

became the custom to present the little bouquets in silvered water tubes as personal expressions of sentiments. Different plants held special meanings in the language of flowers.

Today little herbal bouquets are sometimes carried by brides or given on special days. Made from fresh or dried herbal materials they are decorative potpourris for tabletops or displayed in little vases.

Start with a circle or border of scented leaves such as rose geranium. Add sprigs of herbs to fill the center and accent with flowers. Tie it all together with a bit of ribbon. Add a collar of lace if you like. Make the bouquet from fresh materials and let it dry naturally in a warm dry place. Or start with dried sprigs of herbs and flowers, or combine with fresh parts, and wire it all together. Sprinkle with a bit of orrisroot or other potpourri fixative to preserve the natural scents longer and add a few drops of fragrant oils.

Pomander Balls

Old-fashioned pomander balls are simply fruits studded with whole cloves and dried. They are natural air fresheners and can be hung in a closet to repel moths. But even if they served no practical purposes, pomanders would still be popular, especially during the winter holiday season when they are used as tree ornaments and place-card holders, stacked to form tabletop trees, or given as gifts.

Select perfect pieces of fruit. Oranges are the most popular, but apples, grapefruit, lemons, limes, pears, and even kumquats can be used to make balls of various shapes and sizes. Tradition calls for studding the fruit all over closely with whole cloves. As the fruit dries the skin shrinks and draws the cloves closer together. Today many people who make pomanders add the cloves in rows or patterns or randomly scatter them over the surface leaving some of the fruit skin showing. These areas can be left plain when dried or decorated with small dried flowers or sprigs of herbs or seed head. Always buy good quality, whole cloves that are strongly scented.

Holding the fruit in one hand, make a tiny hole in the skin with a nail, skewer, or any handy sharp instrument. Press a clove all the way into the hole with your finger. Finish the studding the same day you start before the drying begins. Many people roll the studded fruit in orrisroot or ground allspice, cinnamon, cloves or nutmeg, cardamom, or musk.

Place the pomander in a warm, sunny place to dry for a week or so. Turn it from time to time so it will dry evenly. If you are in a big hurry, place the pomander on a baking sheet in an oven that has a pilot light, leaving the door open until the fruit has dried. Do not turn on the heat.

If you plan to hang the pomander, insert a skewer, metal knitting needle, or straight piece of clothes-hanger wire completely through the fruit. As it dries, turn the fruit on the wire regularly to keep it from sticking. When the fruit has dried, thread it with a length of ribbon, yarn, or cord using a crochet hook to work the material through the hole. Tie one end into a knot or bow to keep the ball from slipping off.

Incenses

The burning of herbs and spices freshens stale air and masks unpleasant household or pet odors. You can purchase powders, sticks, and cones in many herbal and spicy scents. Or simply sprinkle powdered herbs and spices on pieces of lighted charcoal in an incense burner or small dish.

A popular recipe originating in the Middle Ages calls for 1 part myrrh, 5 parts frankincense, and 2 parts benzoin mixed together and sprinkled on burning charcoal.

For a subtle long-lasting incense put several pieces of frankincense, myrrh, benzoin, or other fragrant gum in a shallow metal container on a stove burner with the heat set as low as possible. As the gum melts, the clean, slightly spicy fragrance penetrates every corner.

The oily essences of herbs and spices scent homemade wax candles.

Scented Candles

The fragrance of herbs and spices fills the air when candles containing plant parts or their essential oils are burned. Molds for homemade candles can be fashioned from heavy-duty food containers, milk cartons, tin cans, pâté and salad molds, or any other household container that will hold hot wax.

Melt pieces of leftover unscented candles or paraffin wax blocks over hot water in a double boiler. Add several drops of essential oils of an herb or spice, or a combination of two or more; or stir in crushed leaves, petals, and spices. For strongly scented candles combine both oils and plant materials. Add pieces of wax crayons for color.

To make the wick, dip a string that is several inches longer than the mold into the hot wax, leaving a few inches of one end unwaxed. Remove and pull taut to straighten. Tie the unwaxed end to a long pencil or stick, position the string down the center of the mold and rest the pencil or stick across the top of the mold.

Pour the hot wax into the mold around the wick, adding whole leaves, petals, and spices for more fragrance. You may choose to create a layered look of varied colors by pouring small portions of one color, letting it cool and partially harden, then adding another color.

Allow the candle to harden completely before removing from the mold and trimming the wick. If you used a paper mold, just tear it away. Run hot water over the outside of metal molds.

Scented Oils and Perfumes

To make scented oils at home, you will need an odorless corn, olive, or safflower oil, although pure melted lard will do. Gather any fragrant fresh leaves or flowers, or select a dried spice and fill a widemouthed container. Cover with the oil and let stand for 24 hours. Strain the oil into a bowl through two layers of cheesecloth, squeezing to release every drop. Refill the container with more of the fresh or dried material and pour the oil over again. Repeat this straining and pouring every day for 1 to 3 weeks, or until the oil is strongly aromatic. Keep the container in a warm and preferably sunny place throughout the period. When the oil itself is fragrant, strain into little bottles and seal tightly. Homemade fragrance does not last long without one of the expensive perfume fixatives such as musk, civet, ambergris, or castoreum (available from some pharmacies and mail-order suppliers).

Use the oil for bath oil or body scent, or blend with alcohol to create perfume, or use as an additive in potpourri, cosmetics, candles, or soaps.

Herbal massage oil. A very simple infused oil for body massage can be made by adding 4 ounces mixed herbs to 1 quart mixed vegetable oils or fine olive oil. Leave in a warm place for 2 weeks, then strain through cheesecloth and add up to 1 ounce essential oils. Bottle and label. Use soon or refrigerate to prevent spoilage.

For an easy massage oil start with one quart pure vegetable oil of one kind or mixed. Add ½ ounce of your favorite scented essential oils of herbs or spices, one kind or mixed. Shake well and allow to sit for a few days until fragrance develops.

Perfume. To create your own perfume, mix scented oil, one kind or several with compatible fragrances, with an equal portion of unscented, pure ethyl or rectified alcohol in a tightly closed bottle or jar. Shake together very thoroughly every day for about 2 weeks. Then allow the oil and alcohol to separate naturally. Pour off the oil and use for other purposes. Funnel the remaining alcohol, now perfume, into a little bottle and cap tightly.

An alternate method is to start with the pure alcohol instead of oil and pour it over the fresh herbs or flowers. Follow the same procedure used to make scented oil of squeezing and adding fresh ingredients daily until the desired scent is reached. Secure the scent by adding a fixative.

Capture the essence of an herbal or floral garden you've enjoyed in oils and perfumes made at home.

Scented Baths and Splashes

A leisurely bath in herbal water does a lot for the tired body and soul. A simple mixture can be concocted by simmering a handful of fresh or dried herbs, flowers, and spices in a quart of water for 15 to 20 minutes. Let stand for 30 minutes more to fully develop scents, then strain into hot bath water. Or add a sprinkling of essential oils of herbs, spices, or flowers.

You can make herbal sachets of dried leaves and flowers to drop into bath water, hang under the tap while the water draws, or use as a scrubcloth. Just tie up dried herbs and flowers in cheesecloth, muslin, or linen bags. An old French recipe combines leaves of peppermint, sage, rosemary, and thyme with the flowers of chamomile. Other good choices for herbal baths include lemon balm, bay, calendula, comfrey, lavender, pennyroyal, oregano, rose petals or any of the plants suitable for potpourri. Make up several bags at a time and store in an airtight container. For special gifts, pack several herbal bath bags into a basket or package along with a luffa sponge, some herbal soaps, and perhaps a towel set.

After-shower splash. Create an alcohol splash as follows: In a crock or glass container, place fresh or dried leaves of mint, sage, rosemary, lemon balm, seeds of anise or fennel, flowers of lavender or roses, broken pieces of cinnamon or any similar combination of herbs and spices you find appealing. Cover with odorless pure rectified alcohol—not the rubbing kind—available from a pharmacy. Let the mixture stand for about 2 weeks, then filter through a double layer of cheesecloth or coffee filter paper. Bottle one part of the scented alcohol with two parts water.

Shake well and splash on after bathing or showering or have a friend treat you to an herbal rubdown after a hard day's work in your garden. The fragrant alcohol is relaxing to the body and stimulating to the spirit.

Garden Fresh Soaps

Washing with soaps that smell of the herb garden is an invigorating experience. Making soap from bars or leftover scraps of unscented castile or glycerin soaps is quite easy. Just cut the scraps into small pieces and add a little hot water in a saucepan. Pour in a few drops of essential oils of herbs and spices to create a scent you like. Dissolve the soap over a low heat and pour the hot liquid into molds to harden.

Individual salad molds, tin cans, and plastic and paper cartons make good molds for soaps. Large portions of soap can be made in milk cartons and then sliced into bars when hardened. Let your soaps sit for several days in the air to harden before using.

You might pour some of the soap solution into old-fashioned shaving mugs and let harden. A soap-filled mug, along with a shaving brush, is an appreciated gift for friends who don't use an electric shaver.

It is also possible to make your own herbal or spice-scented soaps from scratch. To do so, you will need the following ingredients.

10 pounds lard	6 tablespoons powdered borax
Soft water	½ cup ammonia
4 tablespoons sugar	Essential oils (optional)
2 tablespoons salt	2 cups lye

Spread the lard about 1-inch thick on a board or counter. Press whole or large pieces of fragrant herbs or spices deep into the lard. If these are from your own garden, be sure they have never been sprayed with any kind of chemical pesticide. Cover with cheesecloth to protect from dust. Let stand for 24 hours, then remove the herbs or spices. For a stronger fragrance the process can be repeated.

Place lard in a kettle with 2 quarts of water. Bring to a boil and let cool overnight. Any bits of the herb or spice will settle to the bottom and may be easily removed the next morning.

Harvested herbs may be used to scent refreshing herbal soaps.

Mix the sugar, salt, powdered borax, and ammonia with 1 cup of water in a bowl. If you wish to further heighten the fragrance of the soap, add a few drops of essential oil.

In an outdoor area mix 2 quarts cold water with 2 cups of lye in a stainless steel or enameled pan. Closely follow all the precautions and directions given on the lye package for preparation of lye. Add the sugar, salt, borax, and ammonia mixture.

Slowly add the cool lard to the lye mixture, stirring with a wooden spoon until the newly formed soap is thick and light in color. Pour the thickened soap into a stainless steel or enameled pan or a wooden box lined with a dampened cloth for easy removal.

Let the soap harden. The longer you let it harden, the longer each bar will last. Remove from the mold and cut into portions as desired.

Many herbalists offer plant parts that contain saponins (glucosides that produce a soapy lather) as soap substitutes. You might enjoy trying roots of the California soap plant, soap tree yucca, soapwort, saltbush or Spanish bayonet, or the leaves of papaya and guaiac, as well as fruits of soap pod and wild gourd. They will produce a lather when mixed in warm soft water. People who use them recommend them for washing delicate fabrics. Check nearby herb shops or mail-order sources for availability.

Skin and Hair Care and Mouthwash

A quick check of the ingredients of commercially available products for the skin and hair reveals that herbs are used freely. You can duplicate many of

Beauty products scented with herbs and spices leave aromatic traces in hair and on skin.

these products at home with garden-fresh or dried herbs. There are arguments on both sides as to whether the herbs actually serve any practical purposes in the care of skin and hair. Even if they are no more than a refreshing fragrance, they are welcome additions to these cosmetic aids.

Herbal steam facial. Steaming is one of the best ways to cleanse the skin. The addition of herbs to the hot steam supposedly helps cleanse, stimulate, soothe and tighten the skin, remove impurities, and aid in blemish control. At the very least they are delightful to the senses.

Pour boiling water over fresh or dried herbs in a basin and make a tent of a towel to hold over your head. Let the steam soak your face for 10 minutes or as long as you can stand the heat. Chamomile flowers are the most popular for steam facials. Other possibilities are elder flowers, lime flowers, strawberry leaves, yarrow, lady's mantle, fennel, comfrey, roses, peppermint, and rosemary. Use alone or in combinations.

There are many cleansers and cosmetics that can be made at home using simple ingredients available from a pharmacy or mail-order supplier combined with either fresh or dried herbs.

Cold cream. To make your own cold cream, blend 1 part pure olive oil with 4 parts pure solid vegetable shortening. Add several drops of tincture of benzoin and fragrant herbal oils. An easy alternative starts with commercial *unscented* cold cream; just blend in essential oils.

Cleansing cream. Another cleansing cream calls for melting 1 part white wax with 4 parts avocado or almond oil. Then add 1 part rose or other flower water, 2 parts aloe gel, and a few drops of fragrant oils a little at a time, beating constantly with a fork or in a blender. When mixed, pour into jars.

Rose water cosmetics. Rose water is a fragrant base for several cosmetics (as well as a major seasoning in Turkish cooking). It is easily made at home or may be purchased from gourmet shops, particularly those specializing in Middle Eastern delicacies.

Select the most fragrant roses available. Use only petals from plants that have not been treated with pesticides. Remove the petals and wash them well and pat dry with paper towels.

Rose water may be prepared using distillation equipment from a scientific supply house, but a stove-top still is the easiest and least complicated method. Fill a regular teakettle half full of water and cover the water with a thick layer of rose petals. Securely attach a rubber hose to the spout and place the other end in a glass jar or bottle on the floor. Arrange the hose so that a portion of it is submerged in a pan of ice water en route to the jar. Simmer the kettle over low heat. As the steam rises into the rubber tube, it is cooled by the ice water and condenses into rose water.

Rose skin freshener. Dissolve ¼ teaspoon camphor and 1 teaspoon borax in 1½ teaspoons of tincture of benzoin. Add a cup distilled water and ½ cup rose water. Mix well and bottle.

Skin cleanser. Rose water and glycerin is a traditional skin cleanser. Mix equal portions of glycerin with rose water. Heat just to boiling and store in tightly capped bottles or jars.

Herbal astringents. Herbal astringents are used to close skin pores, remove excess oils, and as aftershave lotions. Begin with an herb extract made by steeping the chosen herb in a jar of pure ethyl alcohol. Suggested astringent herbs include chamomile, bayberry bark, sage, lady's mantle, and yarrow. Strain after one week and add more of the herb. After the second week, strain through doubled cheesecloth and bottle. To each ¼ cup of herb extract, add ½ cup witch hazel, 2 teaspoons glycerine, ½ teaspoon powdered boric acid, and ½ teaspoon tincture of benzoin. For an added tingle add 1 teaspoon peppermint extract. Cap tightly; shake before using.

Hand cream. An excellent hand cream can be created from simple ingredients in 5 minutes time. Start by squeezing a lemon and straining the juice through cheesecloth. Pour juice into a measuring cup and add an equal amount of almond oil. In a small pan put a thin piece of beeswax (about 1 teaspoon). Add a bit of the almond oil that has collected above the lemon juice in the measuring cup. Place over medium heat and gently shake the pot for about 30 seconds. Remove from heat so that the wax melts but does not burn. Add remaining almond-lemon mixture. Heat, shake, and stir with a wooden spoon until the wax has completely melted. Remove from heat. Stir until cool with wooden spoon. Add 1 drop lemon oil for every ounce of cream (about 3 drops). Stir again and transfer to cream jar or bottle. Cap. Shake every few minutes until cream is completely cold.

Mouthwash. A simple breath-freshening mouthwash can be made from a strong peppermint tea or by steeping equal portions of mint, anise, and rosemary in boiling water. Strain and store in a tightly capped bottle.

For a spicy version grind your own blend of cloves, caraway, cinnamon, and nutmeg in a mortar and pestle. Combine the spice mixture with an equal part of dry sherry, add a few drops of tincture of myrrh, peppermint, or lavender and let stand for several days. To use pour a few drops into a glass of water.

Shampoo. Create your own special shampoo blend with a base of liquid castile soap available from a pharmacy. Add a strong infusion or tea of selected herbs and stir together over low heat until the soap melts and the shampoo is well blended. If you wish, add herb or spice essential oils for extra fragrance. To save steps start with a commercial avocado, castile, or coconut shampoo and add the herbal infusion and scents. Store in tightly closed bottles. The following herbs are recommended by many herbalists as shampoo additives:

☐ Light hair. Calendula, chamomile, great mullein or orange flowers, orrisroot, turmeric.

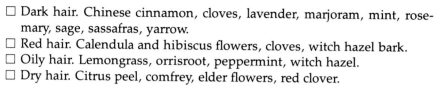

☐ Dark hair. Chinese cinnamon, cloves, lavender, marjoram, mint, rosemary, sage, sassafras, yarrow.

☐ Red hair. Calendula and hibiscus flowers, cloves, witch hazel bark.

☐ Oily hair. Lemongrass, orrisroot, peppermint, witch hazel.

☐ Dry hair. Citrus peel, comfrey, elder flowers, red clover.

Herbal protein shampoo. This special herbal protein shampoo was created by San Francisco herbalist Jeanne Rose.

2 tablespoons Irish moss	4½ cups water
½ cup *each* chamomile and calendula flowers, fresh or dried	¾ cup shaved castile soaplets
¼ cup orange peel, fresh or dried	A few drops of essential oils of your choice dissolved in ½ ounce tincture of
¼ cup orrisroot	benzoin

Mix herbs together and boil in water in an enamel pot for about 5 minutes. Turn off heat and let steep. Pour soap into an enamel bowl. Strain herb water through cheesecloth or muslin into the soap. Gently beat until soap is dissolved, heating if necessary. Pour into quart container, add oils and shake. Cap and label.

Hair rinse. A simple hair rinse can be easily made by adding 1 cup of boiling water to 3 to 4 tablespoons of herbs and simmering gently for several minutes. Strain and blend with 1 cup cold bottled "spring" water. Pour over shampooed hair. Work it through the hair, squeeze out excess, and dry. Use the same herbs as suggested for shampoos, adding any others that have appealing fragrances.

Natural hair colors. The ancient Egyptians used henna to smooth and color the hair. Henna coats each hair shaft to make the hair appear thicker as it smooths the cuticle layer. Many people who want these qualities without changing hair color use natural henna. Colored henna is available in shades from black, through brown, mahogany, to deep red. It is difficult to control the evenness of the color and takes a lot of experimentation at home, so colored henna is best applied by a professional. Herbal cosmeticians recommend natural henna.

If you want to try it, start with about 2 cups henna powder and add hot water to form a thick paste. A teaspoon of vinegar helps release the dye. Stir the paste well and let it stand while you shampoo the hair. When applying henna wear rubber gloves to avoid staining your hands and nails. Wrap the hairline in cotton to prevent dripping. Apply to sections of the hair with a stiff brush, painting both sides of the hair. When completed, cover the head with a plasic bag and keep it on for ½ to 1½ hours. Rinse until water comes clear.

The touch of herbs is the touch of color in makeup you make yourself.

Practitioners of the art of natural cosmetics suggest a wide range of herbal parts for coloring. Natural hair colors for dark hair include crushed walnut shells, sandalwood, redwood bark, brazilwood, and elderberries. To brighten dull dark hair, apply rosemary or southernwood. To brighten light-colored hair apply chamomile, calendula, great mullein leaves, or lemon peel. To darken gray hair make a decoction of sage, bay laurel, marjoram, and wood betony.

Herbal makeup. Herbal makeup adds a natural touch of color to highlight healthy skin. Here are some easy ones for the home herbalist to prepare. Start with small quantities and experiment with the amounts of herbs used to create desired colors. A collection of herbal makeup items, along with skin and hair care products packed into a kit, bag, basket, or tray is a refreshing way to share the harvest of your garden with special friends.

Lipstick. Alkanet root is the basis for a blush or lipstick in a pot. Mix 2 tablespoons of the root in ½ cup sesame oil and let stand for about 2 weeks. Then melt 4 tablespoons beeswax in a saucepan and add the strained oil mixture. Beat until cold and store in small jars.

Eye shadow. Eye shadow can be made by heating 1 part fresh herb to 4 parts pure oil until the oil is well colored. Add 1 part beeswax to the oil and heat until melted. Beat until cold and pack into small containers. For lavender shadow use black malva flowers combined with alkanet. For green eye shadow use parsley. For yellow shadow start with calendula petals. Apply a strong decoction of sage boiled in a black cast iron pot to darken the eyebrows.

Nail polish. A softly colored nail polish can be made from henna powder simply by adding hot water to form a thin paste. Paint onto nails with a small brush and let dry. Rinse with cold water.

Decorating with Herbs and Spices

In addition to the beauty of living herb plants indoors and outdoors, preserved plant forms can be used in many ways to add color and warmth to a home.

Perhaps the easiest way to display garden materials is in bouquets of dried flowers and foliage that have been preserved by one of the methods described on pages 29–33.

Dried bouquets. Especially pretty when dried are leaves of eucalyptus, horehound, lamb's ears, sage, mints, and oregano; the seed pods of dill, fennel, and roses; and flowers of bergamot, calendula, dock, goldenrod, onions, roses, safflower, tansy, and wormwood. Many other plants are attractive when dried. Experiment with the different plant parts and preserving techniques.

Flowers with strong stiff stems will stand just as they are. Others will need lengths of florist's wire attached to the base of the flower, seed head, or the foliage clump. Bend the wire back at the length you want for the stem. Holding the attached blossom or head securely, use your other hand to wrap the remaining length several times around the short remaining stem or foliage clump. For roses, calendulas, and other flowers with fat bases, remove the stems and insert the wire through the base of the flower.

Beginning at the flower or pod base or the end of the foliage, wrap florist's tape tightly to cover the wire, stretching as you wrap downward. A shade of brown or drab green tape looks best with dried flowers and leaves.

Cut a piece of styrofoam to fill the base of the container or basket selected for the bouquet. If necessary secure the foam to the bottom of the container with floral adhesive. If you can see the styrofoam, cover it with dried green moss. Push the flower stems or wires into the foam. A coating of hair spray over the completed bouquet will help keep the dried materials together. To maintain as much color as possible, keep the bouquet away from strong sunlight.

Miniature bouquets. Some people enjoy making miniature bouquets and displaying them underneath a glass dome or inside a deep shadowbox frame.

The little bouquets known as tussie mussies are charming accents for bedside tables, powder rooms, or other small areas. Both tussie mussies and containers of colorful potpourri are decorative as well as practical air fresheners. The little herbal bouquets and potpourri are charming gifts, too. See pages 78–82 for instructions.

Herb and spice wreaths and garlands. A variation of the dried bouquet is the herb and spice wreath for winter holiday decoration. Use a wire wreath frame from the florist as an anchor for sprigs of dried herbs. Wire them to the frame to make a lush base. Gray or silver herb foliage is especially pretty as the base. Add colorful flowers, seed heads and pods, cones, and berries

to complete the design. Keep the color scheme monochromatic, add one complementary or contrasting color, or create a fantasy of mixed hues. The addition of a bow and streamers is a matter of personal taste. For a simpler wreath design select only one type of foliage or seed head and fashion into a circle.

Fragrant herbal wreaths are attractive on doors, windows or walls, especially in dining areas or kitchens. They are equally attractive on tabletops where they can ring candles or a punch bowl.

After the holidays you can hang the wreath near the stove to use the sprigs in cooking. Or you can spray it with hair spray and store it away in a large plastic bag for use again next year. Friends will appreciate wreaths as gifts.

Bay leaf wreath. Much-appreciated holiday gifts are bay leaf wreaths that can be hung in the kitchen and used all year. Wrap a round styrofoam wreath base in velvet ribbon or strips of burlap. Using ordinary straight sewing pins, attach bay leaves thickly over the base, continually overlapping the ends of the leaves to hide it and the pins. Add a flat simple velvet or grosgrain ribbon bow.

Garlands. Instead of turning dried herbs and flowers into wreaths you may enjoy making a long garland to festoon a stairway, mantle, or buffet table. Tie the wired floral and foliage pieces to a long piece of wire or heavy cord cut to any length. Begin with a base of herb foliage, then add flowers, berries, and other decorative accents as in making wreaths.

Garlic braids. Don't forget strings of braided garlic, peppers, and onions (described on page 34) for year-round decorations. They are colorful accents for kitchen and dining areas.

Other Christmas decorations. Sprigs of dried herbs and flowers are charming decorations on a Christmas tree. Tie them into little nosegays and hang them on the tree along with other traditional ornaments. An entire tree can be decorated with dried garden plants. First insert sprays of delicate-looking flowers or seed heads to completely fill in all the spaces between tree branches. Next add colorful flowers, pomander balls, pods, and other dried materials as bold accents. Such a tree takes a lot of dried materials and time, but the results are spectacular and highly aromatic. Use the same idea and techniques to make a small tabletop tree for a party centerpiece.

If you would like a more permanent herbal tree, cover an 18-inch styrofoam cone with ribbon or green moss held in place with fern pins or bent pieces of wire. Cover the cone with delicate dried seed heads or airy flowers. Then add larger flowers and herb sprigs, along with cones and berries for accents. The tree can be sprayed with hair lacquer and stored away in a plastic bag for another year.

Natural Notes and Pictures

Foliage and flowers from the herb garden can be turned into cards and mounted pictures that you will enjoy making, keeping, and giving.

Select perfect leaves and flowers from your garden and press them so they are not touching between sheets of blotting paper or newspaper weighted down by heavy books. Press small blooms whole, but separate the petals of larger or thicker flowers and press each separately. When dry, in about 4 or 5 weeks, gently lift the dry flowers off the pages with tweezers and store the pressed material between sheets of waxed paper until you are ready to make the designs. Dry a large variety of materials this way so you will have good choices when you create projects later.

A flower press. For a more professional way of pressing plant parts, buy a flower press from the hobby store or build your own simple version: Cut 2 pieces of heavy plywood 1-foot square and drill holes an inch from each corner on the diagonal. Cut several sheets of corrugated cardboard and blotting paper to the same size, cutting off the corners to allow room for screws to be inserted through the corner holes.

Opposite: The rich autumnal hues of yarrow, safflowers, dock, cress, and other dried herbs were preserved by hang drying.

Below: Create notecards or illustrate a gardener's diary with pressed flowers.

Arrange the petals, flowers, and leaves on a piece of blotter so the plants do not touch. Cover with another blotter and slip this between a pair of cardboard sheets. Continue until all the plant parts are accommodated, then put the whole stack between the sheets of plywood. Insert 3- to 4-inch bolts in the corner holes and fasten tightly with wing nuts. Store in a warm dry area until the plants are crisp. On top of the refrigerator or the clothes dryer, or on a radiator or heat vent are good places. When the materials are completely dry, remove with tweezers and store between waxed paper.

You can form a design of the petals and leaves on plain notecards and envelopes from the stationery store. Glue each petal, flower, or leaf in place with thinned rubber cement. Burnish by covering with tissue paper and rubbing the surface with your finger or a flat stick. When the glue dries, carefully rub off any excess rubber cement from around the edges of the plant. Smaller versions of notecards make attractive gift tags.

Use the pressed materials to illustrate pages of your garden diary or create a little book of herbs and spices with plant identifications (see instructions below).

Pressed flowers and leaves can be formed into larger designs and glued to artists' mounting board, then framed under glass. An alternate method is to glue the plant pieces directly onto the back side of glass or lucite box frames available from hobby shops. Hang your pictures away from sunlight to preserve the colors of petals and foliage.

The Gardener's Diary

Serious gardeners enjoy keeping a record of plants in the herb garden: sources of seeds or cuttings, location in the garden, culture, plant response, and yearly harvest.

To make the diary distinctive you might want to buy a leather or clothbound book with blank pages. Or cover an inexpensive sketchbook with fabric you like. If you can make a pencil or watercolor sketch of the plant alongside your record page. Or illustrate the plant with its own pressed leaves and petals as previously described.

Natural Dyeing

Strong infusions of almost any herbs boiled in water can be used in coloring natural fabrics: cotton, linen, silk, or, most satisfactorily, wool. Of course the dyes from some plants are more readily absorbed than others by the fibers.

Do not expect the bright colors of synthetic dyes. Natural dyes are subtle. Hues will vary according to where and how the plant grew, the strength of the dye solution, whether the dye is made from fresh or dried plant parts, and the type of mordant (dye-setting compound) used.

Prior to the actual dyeing, it is necessary to treat the fabric in a mordant to set the dye in the fibers. Alum is the most commonly used mordant, but acetic acid, ammonia, chrome, tin, and iron chemicals are also used. The choice of mordant often also influences the color produced.

The dyeing procedure varies with the fabric, plant material, and mordant selected. Our space does not permit detailed instructions, but there are several books devoted to natural dyeing if you wish to pursue the hobby.

Herbal colors

☐ Reds. Alkanet roots, bedstraw roots, bloodroot roots, madder roots, oregano leaves, tea leaves.
☐ Oranges. Henna leaves, lily-of-the-valley leaves, onion skins, sorrel leaves, tansy shoots.
☐ Yellows. Agrimony leaves and flowers, barberry stems and roots, calendula flowers, dyer's broom tops, fenugreek seeds, goldenrod blooms, saffron crocus blooms, St.-John's-wort flowers, turmeric roots, yarrow flowers.

Natural dyes lend subtle shades to yarn.

☐ Violet. Hibiscus flowers, oregano leaves.
☐ Blue. Cornflowers, elecampane roots, hollyhock flowers, wild indigo branches.
☐ Green. Coltsfoot leaves, dyer's broom tops, hyssop leaves, larkspur flowers, onion skins, sorrel leaves, sweet cicely stems and leaves.
☐ Brown. Hibiscus flowers, juniper berries, tea leaves.
☐ Gray. Blackberry shoots.
☐ Black. Barberry leaves, yellow dock roots.

PLANT SELECTION GUIDE

Angelica grows in partial shade, whereas fennel prefers full sun. This list tells you which herbs and spices will flourish in your garden and where.

Thousands of plants that could be classed as herbs and spices are cultivated today. Herbalists often disagree as to which plants should be included in an herb garden. A few purists insist that only the obvious culinary, fragrance, dye, or medicinal plants can be ranked as herbs. Using the more general definition of herbs and spices as plants that produce useful parts for flavoring, fragrances, decorations, or crafts, the plants listed in the following pages represent a selection of herbs and spices suitable for home gardens. The commercial form of most of these herbs is illustrated in the chapter "Commercial Herbs and Spices" (see page 128), in addition to others not recommended for home gardens.

Almost all of the culinary herbs are listed, along with many plants grown for their scents. Some are desirable just for their attractive foliage, flowers, or forms. A few ancient herbs are included purely for historical interest. Those herbs that are strictly medicinal or those that are poisonous have not been included.

This guide describes the size of specific plants that will be useful in designing and planting your landscape. Take note of the light, soil, water, and other cultural requirements to help you determine what to plant where. Remember that these requirements are for *ideal* conditions under which a plant will flourish. Every garden cannot satisfy the optimum requirements of all plants. If a spot in your garden seems close to being ideal, give it a try! Part of the joy of gardening is experimenting and being pleasantly surprised by the results.

Gardeners who are new to herbs will probably elect to start with several less demanding plants and learn to grow those well before moving on to some that take a little more effort. Be sure to select a few that will give drama or color to the garden.

Home gardeners should not expect large harvests from some of these plants. They are included in the list because it will be fun and informative to watch how they grow and contribute to your understanding of herbs and spices. There are many challenges and joys in trying something new, or in the case of many herbs, rediscovering something very old that has been neglected by many modern gardeners.

Agrimony (*Agrimonia eupatoria*)

Also known as cocklebur and church steeples, this 2- to 3-foot high perennial has sets of compound, dark green leaves that smell like apricots. A spike of tiny yellow blossoms rises on a hair stalk in the summer. The flowers turn into a hooked seedpod or cocklebur.

The leaves and flowers may be used as a fragrance, and the leaves will produce a golden yellow dye. Grow agrimony in any soil that stays dry. It prefers full sun but will adjust to some shade. Propagate from seed or by dividing plants in the spring.

Ajuga (*Ajuga reptans*)

Aloe vera (*Aloe barbadensis*)

Angelica (*Angelica archangelica*)

Ajuga (*Ajuga reptans*)

Roots of ajuga or bugleweed can be used to make a black dye. This perennial spreads so fast and thickly that it is often used as a ground cover. Shiny oval leaves form flat rosettes with long runners. Varieties are available with foliage of burgundy or green variegated with pink or white. Spiky flowers are in blue, purple, red, or white.

Grow this highly adaptable plant in any soil in sun or partial shade. To establish as a ground cover, set plants 6 to 12 inches apart. Propagate by cuttings from the ends of runners.

Alkanet (*Anchusa officinalis*)

This biennial herb or short-lived perennial, known also as bugloss, has rough textured, hairy leaves 3 to 6 inches long. The plant grows to 2 feet and bears clusters of blue or purple flowers that taste like cucumber.

The bark of the roots can be used to produce a red dye and is also used to stain wooden furniture a rosewood color. Grow in full sun or partial shade and rich, well-drained soil. Propagate from seed, root division in the spring, or root cuttings in the fall.

Aloe Vera (*Aloe barbadensis*)

The resin from the fleshy leaves of this succulent perennial is a familiar ingredient in cosmetics and skin-care products. The thick succulent leaves, edged with soft spines, grow from the crown of the plant 6 to 24 inches long. When the plant is old, spikes covered with yellow bell flowers may rise from the center.

Aloe survives outdoors only in very mild winter regions. In other areas it should be grown in containers placed where the temperature does not drop below 50°F (10°C). Pot in any standard houseplant soil mix. Let the soil dry out between waterings, especially in the winter. After the first year, fertilize annually with half-strength houseplant food. Propagate by separating the suckers that form around the base.

Angelica (*Angelica* species)

Two species of angelica are of interest to home gardeners. Both are biennial or short-lived perennial members of the carrot family with large, light green leaves and showy clusters of white or greenish flowers on hollow stems. *A. archangelica* grows 4 to 6 feet and is aromatic and celerylike. Similar is *A. atropurpurea*, except the stems and veins of the leaves are purple. Other species of angelica are weedy or poisonous.

Angelica leaves can be used to brew a mild-flavored tea, or add a subtle flavor to fish. The stalks are often candied and used in fruitcakes or enjoyed by themselves.

Grow in partial shade and well-drained, lightly moist soil. The plant will be a perennial if the flower heads are cut off before they set seed. Propagate from seeds, but sow them immediately when they are ripe.

Anise (*Pimpinella anisum*)

Licorice-flavored leaves and seed characterize this slow-growing annual. The seeds are used as a flavoring in cooking and liquors. They are tiny umbrellalike clusters of yellowish blooms. Oval leaves at the base change into three-segment leaves higher up the 18- to 24-inch stems.

Grow anise in full sun and fairly rich, well-drained soil. Propagate by seed. Do not transplant after the plant is established. It is difficult to grow in the north because of its long growing season; start early indoors and leave in pots when carried outside.

Arrowroot (*Maranta arundinacea*)

This tropical perennial should be grown as a greenhouse plant or houseplant unless you live in the warm moist climate of the Gulf coast. The plant grows to a height of 4 to 6 feet and the handsome foliage of shiny, dark green leaves, which may grow to as large as 4 inches across and 1 foot long, make this plant a dramatic addition to any indoor landscape. The small white flowers are unspectacular, but provide a charming counterpoint to the leaves. The rhizomes of selected cultivars are dried and powdered for use as a cooking starch.

Plant in rich, loamy, well-draining soil kept moist most of the year; during the winter months, the soil may be allowed to dry out a little. Keep in a well-lighted place with good air circulation. Be careful not to let it receive direct sun except in the winter months, otherwise the leaves will burn. Water below the level of pebbles in the saucer will help keep the air around the plant humid. Apply a balanced fertilizer once a month during the spring and early summer. Propagate by division.

Artemisia (*Artemisia* species)

Several species are grown for their feathery foliages. In addition to tarragon (*A. dracunculus*), listed separately, an additional species is used as a culinary flavoring.

Southernwood (*A. abrotanum*) has lemon-scented feathery green foliage. The woody perennial grows 3 to 4 feet in height. Flowers are yellowish.

Wormwood (*A. absinthium*), one of the Biblical bitter herbs, was used to flavor absinthe liqueur. It can be highly toxic and is not recommended for home gardens.

Grow artemisias in full sun and dry, poor soil. Propagate from divisions or stem cuttings.

Wormwood (*Artemisia absinthium*)

Asparagus (*Asparagus officinalis*)

Most vegetable-gardening books will give you detailed instructions on growing this delicious vegetable. But in addition to harvesting the stalks, you may also wish to collect the seeds from the late-summer foliage and grind these to brew a tasty, noncaffeinated coffee-substitute. A tea may also be brewed from the chopped-up root of the plant, but you will probably want to try this only with older roots that are diminishing in their production of stalks.

Barberry (*Berberis vulgaris*)

This deciduous shrub can be an attractive addition to a garden. Golden yellow flowers against a light green foliage herald the spring, while in the fall the dark green leaves of summer turn brilliant yellow and shiny red fruits provide the contrast. The cultivar 'Atropurpurea' has purple leaves and fruit. Growing to a height of 7 feet, it makes an excellent hedge with small spines at the base of each leaf cluster. The roots and inner bark can be used to make a yellow dye, and the berries can be harvested for jelly.

Barberry likes moist, well-drained soil, though it can tolerate occasional dryness. Propagate from seeds, layering, or stem cuttings. This species of barberry, as well as *B. canadensis*, should not be planted in grain-growing regions, because the plants are hosts to one stage in the development of a wheat rust.

Basil (*Ocimum basilicum*)

The silky leaves of this bushy annual look creased. A favorite flavoring of cooks in sauces, it can also be a striking border edging. Growing to 2 feet, it has sprinkles of whitish to lavender flowers. The cultivar 'Purpurascens' has vivid purple leaves. The cultivar 'Minimum' (bush basil) is more compact. Keep all basils pinched for fuller growth. Do not fertilize. When harvesting in early summer, if you do not cut the plants all the way back to the ground, they will provide a second crop.

Bay (*Laurus nobilis*)

Bayberry (*Myrica pensylvanica*)

Bedstraw (*Galium verum*)

Bergamot (*Monarda didyma* 'Granite Pink')

Basils grow best in full sun or partial shade. They prefer moderately rich soil that is kept slightly moist. Propagate by seed.

Bay (*Laurus nobilis*)

Sweet bay is an evergreen shrub that will grow into a medium-size tree under favorable conditions. The 2- to 4-inch shiny, dark green leaves are used in flavoring many dishes. The plant produces small yellow flowers followed by black or purple berries.

Seeds take a long time to germinate and cuttings do not always root. It is best to start with a nursery plant. Pot in a container that is comfortable for the rootball. Use any rich well-draining soil mix. Do not let the soil dry out between waterings. Grow in bright light with some shade during the hot part of summer days. It will withstand several degrees of frost, but where winters are harsh, protect in a cool room in winter.

The California bay (*Umbellularia californica*) has a similar flavor and aroma to the Mediterranean bay and is often substituted for it.

Bayberry (*Myrica pensylvanica*)

A deciduous or semi-evergreen shrub with gray berries naturally coated with a wax used in candlemaking, bayberry is a native of North America. It grows to 9 feet tall with dull green, 4-inch aromatic leaves.

Bayberry grows best in poor, sandy soil with only a moderate amount of water. Keep as many roots together as possible when transplanting. Propagate by seeds, layering, or rooting suckers.

Bedstraw (*Galium verum*)

The stems and leaves of this perennial were once grown to stuff mattresses; hence its common name. The root also produces a red dye, though today it is usually grown only for ornamental purposes. Tiny yellow flowers cluster on stems from 1 to 3 feet tall. The leaves are mossy and circle the stems in groups of six to eight, giving a delicate appearance.

Plant bedstraw in full sun or partial shade; it needs only routine garden maintenance. The sprawly plant looks best when staked. Propagate from fresh seed sown in the autumn or root division in the spring.

Bergamot (*Monarda didyma*)

Bee balm and Oswego tea are other common names for this perennial that was the substitute for the tea boycotted by the rebellious patriots at the time of the Boston Tea Party. It grows 3 feet tall and produces shaggy, flaming red, aromatic flowers. Wild bergamot or horsemint (*M. punctata*) is grown for the minty leaves also used in tea and fragrances.

Bergamot does not grow well in warm climates. It tolerates some shade but prefers full sun. Grow it in humus-rich soil that is kept fairly moist. It is slow to start from seed, so buy nursery stock or propagate by dividing plants in the spring. To strengthen the plant cut back flower heads the first year before they bloom. In subsequent years, if the plant is cut down to the ground after the first bloom, it will bloom again in early autumn. Roots are very shallow, so exercise care in weeding. Prune almost to the ground in the fall.

The bark of a mature tree of yellow birch (*Betula alleghaniensis*)

Birch (*Betula* species)

Most people are familiar with these graceful trees, grown primarily as ornamentals. Their distinctive, fissured, sometimes flakey bark can range in color from the familiar whitish gray to reddish brown to almost black. Two species are of interest to the herbalist.

Yellow birch (*B. alleghaniensis*) can grow to 90 feet and has bark that peels in thin flakes ranging in color from yellowish or silver-gray in young trees, to reddish brown on older trunks. The young bark is aromatic and slightly bitter in taste. The cherry or sweet birch (*B. lenta*), which grows to 75 feet, has nonpeeling bark that turns almost black on mature trees. The young bark and twigs are highly aromatic and pleasant tasting; they are now the main source of oil of wintergreen. The young bark and twigs of both species may be used to brew a tea.

Most birches like moist sandy soil. They do best in northern climates, though some species (*B. lenta* among them) adapt well to warmer temperatures. Propagate by seed, layering, or greenwood cuttings in a greenhouse.

Blackberry (*Rubus* 'Olallie')

Blackberry (*Rubus* species)

These plants provide a triple bonus for the gardener: in addition to the delectable fruit, their tender young shoots can be used to prepare a gray dye and their leaves a mild tea. Blackberries are easy to grow in most good, well-draining soil. They should be protected by a mulch or covered with earth during the winter where temperatures are low. Cut canes that have been harvested back to the ground and keep suckers pruned back so that the canes do not develop into a thicket. A sparing application of a complete fertilizer is necessary only if the soil is poor. Propagation is best achieved by suckers or root cuttings. The choice of cultivar is largely dependent on your climate; ask at your local nursery for a recommendation of varieties performing well under your conditions.

Bloodroot (*Sanguinaria canadensis*)

Bloodroot (*Sanguinaria canadensis*)

This easily grown perennial produces a large, showy, white (sometimes tinged with pink) flower on a 6- to 8-inch stalk in the spring along with its single, large, fan-shaped leaf. Bloodroot prefers a light soil, but will grow just about anywhere, in sun or shade. It is best transplanted in August when the leaf begins to die down, but it can be moved at almost any time, even just before blooming. Propagate by division of older plants in the late summer or fall. Bloodroot works well as a rock garden plant, as an edging, or planted in clusters in a woodland setting. The root produces a red dye.

Boneset (*Eupatorium perfoliatum*)

Despite what the common name implies, this herb was not used to set fractures, but was used to relieve a virus once known as breakbone fever. This hardy perennial grows from 3 to 5 feet tall in moist, rich, well-drained soil. Though it prefers full sun, it will still perform well in partial shade. The hairy stem is bracketed by opposed sets of roughly textured leaves which join at the base, completely surrounding the stem. The fluffy white clusters of flowers at the tip of the plant bloom in late summer and autumn. A relative, Joe-Pye weed (*E. purpureum*) grows twice as tall and features purplish nodes and purplish to pinkish flowers. Both species can be propagated from seeds or division. The leaves are used to brew a tea.

Joe-Pye weed (*Eupatorium purpureum*)

Borage (*Borago officinalis*)

A highly ornamental annual, borage grows to a height of 2 feet. Gray-green leaves close to the ground set off star-shaped, bright blue or purple flowers. Since the flowers droop, it is best planted on a slope where it can be seen to best advantage from below. The foliage tends to sprawl so it requires lots of garden space. It does not transplant well but germinates easily. Sow three times at 4-week intervals to stretch your harvest.

The refreshing cucumber flavor of the stem, leaves, and flowers recommend it as a salad herb, or a hot or cold tea. The flowers may also be candied.

Borage grows in full sun or partial shade and adapts to any soil, but prefers poor soil. Water moderately and allow soil to dry out a bit between waterings. Propagate by seed.

Boxwood (*Buxus* species)

Though not itself an herb, boxwood has become an indispensable part of the formal herb garden. The evergreen shrubs are used as borders and hedges to define patterns. Although boxwood will grow large in mild climates, in the herb garden it is kept small and compact through regular clipping. Once established, the plants live for many years. There are gardens with plants still growing that were started during the American colonial period.

Common boxwood (*B. sempervirens*) has dark green, glossy leaves that are about 1½ inches long. The cultivar 'Suffruticosa' is a dwarf that is often used in the herb garden. If you live in a cold climate, your best choice is the Japanese boxwood (*B. microphylla*), especially the variety *koreana*.

Boxwoods tolerate partial shade and need well-drained soil. Prune after new growth has formed in late spring. Keep dead leaves and twigs cut out from the inside. Propagate by cuttings or division.

Burdock (*Arctium lappa*)

This shrubby perennial is usually treated as an annual if its roots are to be harvested, but it can also provide a handsome screen (growing to 10 feet) if kept under control and not allowed to self-seed. The plant branches extensively, with long leaves that are fuzzy-white underneath, and produces small clusters of purplish red flowers in the spring. Burdock is prized as a root vegetable in Japan where it is known as *gobo*, though in the West it is traditionally used as a mild flavoring. If treated as an annual, sow seeds in deep loose soil in spring for a fall harvest, or in the fall for a spring harvest. It tolerates partial shade and requires only a moderate amount of water, but should not be allowed to dry out.

Burnet (*Poterium sanguisorba*)

Too often overlooked, burnet is a perennial with rounded, toothed, lacy leaves that hug the ground. Flower stems rise above the leaves to a height of 2 feet. Flowers are in unusual tight, rounded clusters and rose colored. Keep the flower heads cut back for almost continuous summer bloom. The tender young leaves are a delightful accompaniment to green salads. Do not let them get higher than 4 or 5 inches or they will be tough.

Plant burnet in full sun and well-drained soil that is kept fairly dry. Propagate from seeds or division in the spring.

Calendula (*Calendula officinalis*)

Shakespeare and ancient herbalists called them marigolds. Now they are known mostly by their botanical name or as pot marigolds. Calendulas enjoy a long flowering season. In warm regions they bloom in winter and spring; elsewhere in summer and fall. This annual has angular, branched, hairy stems to 2 feet high with 4-inch orange flowers. The many cultivars produce flowers ranging from pale yellow to deep orange.

Borage (*Borago officinalis*)

Boxwood (*Buxus* species)

Burdock (*Arctium* species)

Burnet (*Poterium sanguisorba*)

The garden color that calendulas provide can also be brought indoors as freshly cut flowers, or the petals can be sprinkled over a salad or dessert. Calendula petals are often used as a substitute for saffron and may be used to prepare a yellow-orange dye.

Most gardeners start with transplants from the nursery, though seeds germinate very quickly. Grow in full sun and ordinary soil with routine watering. Keep flower heads cut back for continuous bloom. Propagate from seed.

Calendula (*Calendula officinalis*)

Caper Bush (*Capparis spinosa*)

The pickled flower buds of the caper bush are the familiar capers known to cooks. The plant is a spiny, small (to 3 feet) shrub that tends to straggle. In warm regions the plant can be grown as a perennial outdoors. In some regions with a long enough growing season it can be treated as a tender annual; otherwise the caper bush needs the warmth of a greenhouse to produce usable buds. The bush needs full sun, poor but well-drained soil, and little water. Propagate by cuttings or seeds.

Caraway (*Carum carvi*)

The carrotlike lacy leaves of this biennial grow in a beautiful rosette to 15 inches the first year. Sturdy shoots to 2 feet high are topped with umbels of white flowers the second summer. The tender young leaves can be used as a flavoring in salads or soups, but caraway is primarily grown for its seeds, which are used to flavor breads, cakes, cheese, pies, salads, and soups. If seed production is not a priority, the flower stalks—either freshly cut or dried—are effective in arrangements.

Caraway (*Carum carvi*)

Grow in full sun and fairly dry, well-drained soil. Caraway seeds germinate easily, and you should let some plants self-seed each year. Seedlings do not transplant easily because of a long taproot.

Carnations and Pinks (*Dianthus* species)

The clovelike odor and visual charm of carnations and pinks has kept them among the ranks of herb garden plants through the centuries as a fragrant source of perfume. Sizes range from low-growing miniature pinks with small flowers to the tall florist's carnation. The many varieties of pinks provide flowers in every shade from pink to red, as well as white. The carnation species (*D. caryophyllus*) also comes in shades of yellow, orange, lavender, and purple. Both pinks and carnation varieties are available with striped or variegated petals. The evergreen foliage is most often gray-blue.

Most dianthus species are perennial, though 2-year-old plants give the best bloom. All need full sun, although some will bloom in partial shade. The soil should be well-drained, slightly alkaline, and kept slightly moist. Carnations are most successful in warmer climates or as greenhouse plants. Propagate by division, stem cuttings, or layering.

Carob (*Ceratonia siliqua*)

This handsome evergreen tree, a native of the arid Mediterranean region, can be grown only in areas where frost is nonexistent or negligible. A slow grower, it can reach a height of 50 feet in any well-drained soil. It needs little water, though two or three irrigations during the summer will help the development of young trees and increase the harvest of older trees. The flowers are small and red and inconspicuous, but the distinctive, long brown seedpods in the fall signal the time to harvest. The pulp surrounding the seeds is used to make carob flour, a chocolatelike flavoring for desserts.

Catnip (*Nepeta cataria*)

Felines love this 2- to 3-foot perennial. Downy, heart-shaped leaves have toothed edges; it is a good candidate for a gray and silver garden. White or

Pinks (*Dianthus plumarius*)

Catnip (*Nepeta cataria*)

Chamomile (*Chamaemelum nobile*)

Chervil (*Anthriscus cerefolium*)

Chicory (*Cichorium intybus* 'Large-Rooted Madgeburg')

lavender flower spikes grow in midsummer. The plants should be cut back each year to avoid a straggly appearance; a harvest in July will usually result in a second harvest in the autumn. The leaves can be brewed for a pleasant tea. The cultivar 'Citriodora' has lemon-scented leaves.

Catnip grows in either full sun or partial shade and light, rich soil. Keep evenly moist. Propagate by seed, cuttings, or division in the spring. Protect small plants from cats until well established.

Cayenne *see* Peppers

Cedar, Red (*Juniperus virginiana*)

This North American evergreen is extensively grown as an ornamental tree, but the distinctive fragrance of the bark and wood is of particular interest to the herbalist. While not a true cedar, it is the source of the fragrant wood used in cedar chests. It prefers loamy soil kept slightly moist, but it will also grow well under rather dry conditions in rocky or gravelly ground. There are a multitude of cultivars with differing growth habits (prostrate, shrubby, tall), growth rates, coloring of foliage (light to dark green). Propagation from seed is very slow (from 2 to 3 years), and cuttings nursed under glass are problematic; small plants purchased from a nursery are your best bet.

Celery (*Apium graveolens* var. *dulce*)

Most books on raising vegetables can give you detailed instructions on growing celery. In warm areas, however, consider not harvesting a couple of plants and letting them remain all winter in the garden; they will reward you with a large quantity of seeds to use as flavoring.

Chamomile (*Chamaemelum nobile*)

A carpet or walkway of fragrant chamomile is an herb garden tradition. This evergreen perennial forms a soft spreading mat of fine foliage about 3 inches high. Twelve-inch high, small daisylike flowers dot the plant in summer. They make a delicious tea.

To establish chamomile, start from seed or buy seedlings. Set in full sun or partial shade in light, well-drained but moist soil. If you need to confine this fast-spreading plant, sink header boards around the area to a depth of 6 inches. If grown as a ground cover, occasional clippings with a mower will keep it controlled and lush.

For container gardening, plant in a large flat tray. Propagate by seed or division in the spring.

Chervil (*Anthriscus cerefolium*)

This sweet aromatic annual, like a milder version of parsley, grows from 1 to 2 feet tall. Keep the flower buds clipped to encourage the growth of the fernlike foliage. Hot weather causes chervil to go to seed quickly; plan on spring or autumn crops.

Seeds germinate easily. Sow seeds in place in the garden in filtered shade and fairly rich soil that is kept slightly moist. Seedlings do not transplant easily; plants will self-seed if allowed to bloom.

Chia *see* Sage

Chicory (*Cichorium intybus*)

A perennial grown as an annual, chicory root, when dried and roasted, provides a slightly bitter additive or substitute for coffee. Resembling a parsnip, it is cultivated in much the same manner. Sow seeds in spring in deeply prepared soil rich in organic matter. Thin the seedlings to about 18 inches apart and keep the plants well cultivated. The roots take about 5 months to mature and are harvested in the fall.

If the roots are dug and then forced in sand, the resulting foliage is known as witloof or Belgian endive. When buying seeds, do not confuse this plant with *C. endivia* (endive) which produces slightly bitter salad greens.

Chili Peppers *see* Peppers

Chinese Chives (*Allium tuberosum*)

Known also as *gow choy, chung fa*, or *yuen sai*, this pungent version of chives has a slight garlic taste. When harvesting cut foliage off at the ground. Grow in full sun or partial shade in well-drained soil kept slightly moist. Propagate by seed or division.

Chives (*Allium schoenoprasum*)

Chives are perennial herbs that grow in clumps with slim grasslike leaves to 10·inches. Refrain from snipping only the growing tips as is the practice with most other herbs. The foliage becomes tough unless clipped close to ground several times during the growing season.

Chives prefer full sun and rich soil, but tolerate partial shade and a lighter soil mix. Keep fairly moist. Propagate by seeds or division.

Chives (*Allium schoenoprasum*)

Chrysanthemum (*Chrysanthemum coronarium*)

Both the young leaves and flower heads of garland chrysanthemum or crown daisies are used to flavor oriental dishes. The plant grows from 1 to 3 feet tall with small flowers of yellow shading to white. Give it the routine care of annual flowers in full sun. Propagate from seeds.

Citrus (*Citrus* species)

Both the flowers and fruits of citrus plants are valued by herb and spice gardeners. The flowers are used in fragrances and additionally for their astringent qualities in cosmetics. The peel of the fruit is used to impart a tangy flavor in all manner of cookery. Pomander balls, cloves combined with whole fruits, impart a traditional fragrance to the winter holiday season.

Dwarf varieties of lemons, limes, and oranges can be grown in containers for easy winter protection in cold regions. Greenhouse gardeners discover citrus plants to be adaptable and productive. Subtropical gardeners can add the plants to the outdoor garden.

Grow citrus in full sun and slightly acid soil that is well drained. Water deeply once a week during hot summer months. Provide additional humidity and more frequent watering when grown in containers. Fertilize with nitrogen in late winter, early summer, and late summer. Prune in early spring to maintain desirable size and shape. Propagate from seeds or cuttings.

Dwarf orange (*Citrus* species)

Coffee (*Coffea arabica*)

Expect a good experience but not a crop from growing the coffee tree at home. Prune its growing tips to develop a compact shrub or small tree (to 15 feet) with glossy, dark green leaves. Spring brings fragrant white flowers followed by bright red fruits (containing the coffee beans) in the summer.

Grow coffee in bright indirect light. Keep above 60°F (16°C) in winter and treat it as you would other indoor houseplants. If leaves yellow, feed with an acid-type fertilizer. Propagate from cuttings of ripe wood.

Comfrey (*Symphytum officinale*)

Known also by the colorful names knit-bone and black-wort, comfrey is a perennial that grows as tall as 3 feet. Large hairy leaves measure up to 20 inches long. Comfrey produces drooping, bell-like flowers in white, yellow, mauve, or blue over a long season. Keep the flowers cut if you want to encourage more leaf growth. The root and the leaves may be used to brew a slightly medicinal-tasting tea.

Coffee (*Coffea arabica*)

Right: Comfrey (*Symphytum officinale*)

Far right: Coriander (*Coriandrum sativum*)

Cornflower (*Centaurea cyanus*)

Costmary (*Chrysanthemum balsamita*)

The plant prefers full or partial shade. Plant in fairly rich soil that is kept moist. Propagate from root cuttings or division.

Coriander (*Coriandrum sativum*)

This annual grows quickly to 12 to 30 inches high. Oval leaves with serrated edges are along the main stems; more deeply cut, feathery leaves are produced on side branches. Flowers bloom in parasol-shaped clusters of pinkish white. If you want only leaves, known as cilantro or Chinese parsley, sow seeds every 2 weeks for a continuous supply; harvest when the plants are 8 to 10 inches high. The spice coriander is the pungent dried mature seed of the plant.

Plant in full sun or partial shade and moderately rich, well-drained soil. Propagate by seeds.

Cornflower (*Centaurea cyanus*)

Also known as bachelor's-button, this hardy, easy-to-grow annual will provide charming spots of color in your garden. Growing 1 to 2 feet tall, the long slender leaves rise from the crown, and equally long, naked stems support the brilliant blue flowers. Plant clusters of seeds in a light, moderately rich soil in full or partial sun; they can be forgiving, but do not let them dry out too often or for too long. Plants will continue to bloom until the first frost and will self-seed and reappear the following spring. The dried flower petals are used to make a blue dye.

Costmary (*Chrysanthemum balsamita*)

Also known as alecost and bibleleaf, this weedy perennial has soft, aromatic, 7-inch leaves with scalloped edges. Erect flower stems with button-like yellow flowers grow to 3 feet. Cut back leggy stems for fuller plants. The leaves were once used as a flavoring in beer, but they are now used to add fragrance to sachets and potpourris.

Costmary can be grown in full sun or partial shade and any well-drained soil. Shady exposures result in fewer blooms. Propagate by division.

Cumin (*Cuminum cyminum*)

Seeds of cumin plants are collected for their pungent flavor. This annual is good for edging as it grows only 6 inches high. Small pink or white blooms develop tiny seeds.

Plant cumin in full sun and well-drained soil. It must have at least 3 months of hot weather to mature. If your growing season is short, start seed indoors to get a head start. Propagate from seed.

Dandelion (*Taraxacum officinale*)

The challenge here is learning to think of dandelion as a useful part of the garden, not just a lawn weed. Confine dandelion to raised beds and your attitude towards it as a pest may vanish.

Leaves of the newer cultivated varieties are tastier than the wild form and many seed companies offer them. Young leaves may be boiled as greens or used to brew a slightly bitter tea, the flower heads yield dandelion wine, and the roasted and ground root can be used as a coffee additive.

Dandelions are a cool-weather crop and can be planted for very early picking and again for fall harvest. During hot summer weather they produce tough foliage. Plant in full sun in any kind of soil. Needless to say, propagation is by seeds.

Dill (*Anethum graveolens*)

This familiar annual with light green, feathery foliage grows to a height of 3 feet. Tiny greenish yellow flowers form in parasol-shaped clusters atop the stems. Both the mild-flavored foliage and the more strongly flavored seeds are used as flavorings.

Full sun is essential for dill. Any well-drained soil with routine watering proves satisfactory. Propagate by seeds sown in place in the garden; plants do not transplant well. Self-seeds easily.

Dill (*Anethum graveolens*)

Dittany of Crete (*Origanum dictamnus*)

White, wooly-haired round leaves cover this small shrub that grows to 1 foot. Long-lasting purple flower bracts support tiny pink blooms. Dittany makes a compact border edging, and the flowers may be used to brew a mild sweet tea.

This ancient herb needs full sun, well-drained soil, and little water. An excellent container plant, it should be protected from frost. Propagate by easily rooted stem cuttings taken in the summer.

Dyer's Broom (*Genista tinctoria*)

Besides its obvious utility as an undemanding but showy ornamental, the yellow flowering tops of dyer's broom, if cut in June or July, will yield a brilliant yellow dye. Another common name, dyer's greenwood, refers to its ability to turn blue wool green.

This broom prefers a mild climate, but in marginal areas it can survive if planted in a sheltered location or given some protection during winter. The shrub thrives in a sunny dry location and grows to 3 feet in height. Propagate from seeds, ground layering, or softwood cuttings.

Another species of broom, *G. villarsii*, is more frost-resistant and is an attractive, though lower-growing shrub. The flowers also produce a yellow dye.

Dittany of Crete (*Origanum dictamnus*)

Elderberry (*Sambucus canadensis*)

A native of North America, this species of elder will provide an effective mass planting of shrubs growing to 8 feet high and provides the herbalist and cook with a number of useful parts. Elder leaves and flowers have long been ingredients in the treatment of dry or inflamed skin; the chopped leaves can be used to make a mildly flavored tea; tender green shoots can be boiled as a spinachlike green; and the fruits can be made into jams or jellies and, of course, the renowned elderberry wine. Along with this bounty, you have the beauty of flat heads of white flowers in early summer and the resulting clusters of purplish black fruit 2 or 3 months later.

Elders prefer moist rich soil and weather northern winters with ease. There are several cultivars available, selected for differing variegations of the leaves or for producing large amounts of fruit. To set fruit, the shrub needs cross-fertilization, so two or more different cultivars or plants grown from seed should be planted in the garden. Propagate from seeds, or preferably from cuttings, division, or suckers.

Dyer's broom (*Genista tinctoria* 'Plena')

Elecampane (*Inula helenium*)

Bright yellow flowers similar to sunflowers (though smaller—2 to 4 inches

Elderberry (*Sambucus* species)

Elecampane (*Inula helenium*)

Eucalyptus (*Eucalyptus citriodora*)

Sweet fennel (*Foeniculum vulgare*)

in diameter) top this coarse but robust perennial that grows to a height of 4 to 6 feet. With little or no branching, large leaves with fuzzy undersides alternate up the stem of the plant. The root yields a distinctive bitter flavoring used in liquors, as well as producing a blue dye.

Grow in full sun and ordinary soil with routine watering, though they may be kept evenly moist. Propagate by seeds or division in the spring.

Eucalyptus (*Eucalyptus* species)

Native primarily to Australia, this genus consists of more than five hundred species well adapted to mild climates. These fast-growing evergreens range in size from shrubs to towering trees, require little maintenance or water once they are established, and will grow in almost any soil. Besides their use as a garden ornamental, the strongly scented leaves of some species can provide a woodsy aroma to potpourris and sachets, and glycerin-dried foliage can add verve to any dried arrangement.

E. dives, a medium-size tree, and *E. dumosa*, a shrub or small tree, produce a large amount of the menthol-scented oil in their leaves; *E. citriodora*, an elegant medium-size tree, produces lemon-scented leaves. *E. polyanthemos*, or silver-dollar tree, has round, gray-green unscented leaves. *E. ficifolia* and *E. preissiana* have splashy red and yellow flowers respectively. Propagate by seeds.

Fennel Flower (*Nigella sativa*)

Spicy seeds that smell like nutmeg are produced in late summer by this annual, known also as black cumin or love-in-a-mist. It is a welcome addition to the herb garden with delicate foliage that resembles sweet fennel, but is not a relative. Small blue flowers top each 1½-foot stem in summer, followed by the seed pods.

Plant nigella in full sun and well-drained soil. Each plant produces only a few seeds, so plant generously. Propagate by sowing seed in place in the garden, since it does not transplant successfully.

Fennel, Sweet (*Foeniculum vulgare*)

A tender perennial that is usually grown as an annual, sweet fennel reaches 3 to 5 feet on bright green hollow stems. It has narrow feathery leaves and flat clusters of golden flowers. Both the foliage and stems are used in cooking to impart a sweet aniselike flavor.

Sow seeds in place in the garden or in large containers since fennel does not transplant well. Grow in full sun and light, well-drained soil. Propagate by seeds.

Fenugreek (*Trigonella foenum-graecum*)

These small annuals resemble a spare, erect (to 2 feet) clover and are valued for their seeds which are used as a main ingredient in curry powder, a maplelike flavoring in desserts, as a tea, and to produce a yellow dye. Fenugreek likes a sunny location with loamy, well-drained soil that is kept well cultivated. Plant seeds in the garden after frost is past. Mature plants will produce small white flowers in about July, and the seedpods, which resemble long string beans, will begin to form about 6 weeks later. Harvest the seedpods when they have turned brown, about 4 to 5 months after planting of seeds. Propagate from seeds.

Foxglove (*Digitalis purpurea*)

Few plants in the herb garden are more spectacular than foxglove. From a dramatic rosette of large gray-green leaves, flower spikes tower to 5 feet and are lined with trumpet blossoms of pure white, through yellows, pinks, and red, to purple. Buds open gradually from bottom to top. Foxglove is a hardy biennial and blooms do not appear until the second year. Cutting the flower spikes back in early summer after the initial bloom will often encourage a second flowering late in the season.

The plant was important in early herb gardens for its medical properties. Today it is grown for its beauty.

Plant in full sun or partial shade in well-drained soil. Routine garden care is sufficient. The plant is not recommended for areas with high summer humidity. Protect the plants during their first winter with a light mulch. Propagate from seed; if blooms are not cut back, plants will self-seed.

Foxglove (*Digitalis purpurea*)

Garlic (*Allium sativum*)

The common garlic is a perennial bulb that reaches a height of 2 to 3 feet. Long narrow leaves sheath the flower stalk topped by a ball-shaped cluster of white or lavender blooms. Single bulbs multiply during the growing season into the familiar clusters of bulblets or cloves.

Garlic needs full sun and rich, well-drained soil. Propagate by dividing the bulbs.

Gas Plant (*Dictamnus albus*)

Among the most curious events in nature is the vapor produced by this perennial in hot weather that will burst into flame when a lighted match is held near the foliage. Also known as burning bush and false dittany, it is a bushy plant that grows to a height of 3 feet. The leaves are dark and leathery and arranged in pairs. Delicate pink or white blooms with reddish filaments and green anthers begin appearing when the plant is a few years old. Both leaves and blossoms give off a slight lemon odor when crushed. The leaves may be used to brew a refreshing tea.

Gas plant tolerates partial shade but prefers full sun. Prepare a deep well-drained soil for its extensive root system. Provide routine plant maintenance. Do not be dismayed when the plant dies down in late fall; like most other perennial herbs it will come back each spring. Propagate from seed sown when ripe.

Gas plant (*Dictamnus albus*)

Geraniums, Scented (*Pelargonium* species)

Among the most fragrant of all the plants in the herb garden are the scented geraniums. These tender shrubby plants grow from 2 to 4 feet tall. Scents are released by hot sun on the leaves or by touching them. Foliage come in a variety of forms, from small, delicate, fernlike leaves to large rounded ones, in many shades of green, and many patterns of variegation. The flowers of most are small but colorful in shades of rose. Leaves may be used as a garnish with foods or added to sachets and potpourris.

The numerous varieties include the following scents: almond (*P. quercifolium*); apple (*P. odoratissimum*); apricot and strawberry (*P. scabrum*); lemon (*P. crispum, P. × limoneum*); lime (*P. × nervosum*); nutmeg (*P. × fragrans*); peppermint (*P. tomentosum*); and rose (*P. capitatum, P. graveolens*).

Give scented geraniums the advantage of full sun. They enjoy light, well-drained soil that stays slightly dry. However, if too dry, they will shed their lower leaves. Plants in containers need half-strength fertilizer every 2 weeks when flowering, monthly during the rest of the year, and bloom best when slightly pot-bound.

Although geraniums have a tendency to get leggy, pinching the growing tips will help train the plants to grow bushier and fuller. They may also be lightly pruned in early spring after the last frost. Propagate by root and stem cuttings.

Scented geranium (*Pelargonium* species)

Germander (*Teucrium chamaedrys*)

Gardeners value germander as a ground cover or edging for formal designs. This dwarf shrub grows in clumps from 6 to 18 inches tall and spreads quickly along creeping roots. Leaves are dark green, shiny ovals with

Germander (*Teucrium chamaedrys*)

scalloped edges. Summer flowers appear in pink whorls where leaves join the stems. The leaves may be used to brew a mild-flavored tea.

Grow in full sun or partial shade and well-drained, fairly rich soil. Spring pruning keeps the plants bushy and lush. Propagate from stem cuttings, root division, or seeds.

Ginger (*Zingiber officinale*)

The showy source of ginger root is a 3- to 4-foot high, bushy plant with long leafstalks. Flowers are produced in a conelike cluster of overlapping bracts. In its natural tropical environment the stalks wither after flowering and the new growth extends the rhizome, which is the part used in cooking. Grow ginger outdoors in summer months or year-round as an indoor or greenhouse container plant.

To start a ginger plant obtain fresh roots from a market or an Oriental food shop. Plant roots with the sprout end up and eyes at soil level. Use rich, moist soil in a pot (or in the ground if you live where summer days are hot). Ginger needs good drainage, partial shade, and humidity. Protect it from high winds and low temperatures.

After the plant matures it will produce new sprouts around its base. Dig up one of these sprouts and you will find a tender new growth of root with a much subtler, fresher taste than the roots sold in the market. The young sprouts are also edible and prized by Chinese and Japanese cooks.

Ginseng (*Panax quinquefolius*)

Five thousand years ago, the Chinese emperor Shen-nung was the first to praise the restorative and healthful properties of this plant. As the name of the genus implies, it was and continues to be used by Chinese herbalists as a panacea for all manner of ills. Whether or not the sometimes extravagant claims of some herbalists are true, tea made from the leaves, flowers, or powdered roots provide a refreshing drink.

Ginseng is a hardy perennial that should be grown in well-drained, light, friable loam that is kept shaded and moist. A single stem rises from the root with a whorl of leaves, and is topped in the spring at about 1 to 2 feet by a ball-shaped cluster of greenish white flowers, which becomes a cluster of bright red berries in the fall.

Be patient; the roots are not considered mature until the plant is 5 to 7 years old. Propagation is by seed; plant them 1-inch deep as soon as they ripen in September and you will have seedlings the following spring. If allowed to dry, the seeds may take as long as 2 years to germinate.

Goldenrod (*Solidago canadensis* 'Golden Baby')

Goldenrod (*Solidago* species)

These tall and slender perennials have been favorites of gardeners in herbaceous borders for many years. Growing from 3 to 5 feet high, bright green leaves branch up the main stalk to clusters of small golden yellow flowers at the top. The leaves of sweet goldenrod (*S. odora*) give off an odor of anise when bruised and are used to brew a mild-flavored tea. The flowering tops of all species will produce a yellow dye, or may be dried for arrangements.

Goldenrod likes full sun, though it takes partial shade, and needs little water in only moderately good soil. Blooming in summer or early fall, the stalk dies down to the ground in winter. Propagate from seed (blooms will appear only after the second year) or division in the spring or fall.

Good-King-Henry (*Chenopodium bonus-henricus*)

The large arrow-shaped leaves of Good-King-Henry or English mercury are often eaten as a substitute for spinach. This perennial grows to a height of 30 inches with yellowish blooms at the end of the leafstalk. Early shoots are sometimes eaten in the same manner as asparagus. Cover them with leaf mold to keep them white and tender as they grow.

Good-King-Henry (*Chenopodium bonus-henricus*)

Plant the herb in partial shade and well-drained soil. Feed with any balanced fertilizer to promote growth and refrain from harvesting many leaves until the third year. Propagate by seeds or root division.

Great Mullein (*Verbascum thapsus*)

This hardy biennial can provide a dramatic accent to a herbaceous border with little effort on the part of the gardener. The woolly, gray-green foliage forms in large (up to 2 feet) rosettes, from the center of which grows the tall (to 6 feet) flower stalk with smaller leaves surmounted by a profusion of yellow flowers. Mullein grows in the poorest soil in a sunny and dry location and requires no cultivation and little water. It achieves its best effect in massed plantings and is a good choice for a gray and silver garden or a hard-to-reach sunny slope. A single first-year rosette planted in a 6-inch pot makes an engaging houseplant. The cut and dried leaves and flowers are used to brew a mild flavored tea. Propagate by cuttings, division, or seeds; it self-seeds very easily and care must be taken to cut flower stalks at the peril of having thick mats of mullein seedlings throughout your garden.

Other species you might wish to try are *V. blattaria*, or butterly mullein, which is not quite as tall and gives a more delicate impression; and *V. phoeniceum*, or purple mullein, also somewhat smaller and with purple or red flowers.

Great mullein (*Verbascum thapsus*)

Heliotrope (*Heliotropium arborescens*)

Let your nose be your guide at the nursery in choosing plants of this half-hardy perennial for the garden. While most have delightful vanillalike fragrances, a few have no scent. Plants grow from 1 to 3 feet tall or more, and must be pinched back to keep them bushy beginning when they are only 4- to 5-inch seedlings. Tiny flowers appear in clusters varying from white to dark purple with shades of rose and lavender in between.

Grow heliotrope in full sun, in a rich soil that is kept moist at all times. Indoor or greenhouse container-grown plants may be subject to aphids and red spider mites. Propagate by seed or layering.

Heliotrope (*Heliotropium arborescens*)

Hen-and-Chickens (*Sempervivum tectorum*)

This succulent perennial, also known as houseleek, has been grown with other herbs through the centuries. Its medical attributes and the superstition of its protective qualities against thunder and lightning have faded, but the plant retains its popularity due to its attractive shape. Thick, light green leaves form a rosette that produces small offshoots around the base. The mother plant dies when flower shoots appear from the center. Young plants continue to grow. Many hybrids and cultivars are offered; variables include the size of the plant and colors at the base and tip of the leaves.

Houseleeks need full sun and fast-draining soil. Let the soil go nearly dry during winter months while the plant rests. Propagate by removing the small offshoots.

Henna (*Lawsonia inermis*)

A handsome slender shrub, henna is suited for cultivation only in warm coastal regions. Usually about 6 to 10 feet fall, it prefers a sunny, well-drained location and only a moderate amount of water. During the summer it produces many rose-colored fragrant flowers; there are also varieties that produce white or deep red flowers. The flowers are used for their fragrance, and the dried and powdered leaves are mixed with water to form an orange dye often used in cosmetics.

Hibiscus (*Hibiscus rosa-sinensis*)

The flowers of this evergreen shrub are its salient point: large deeply colored petals form a cup around the projecting stamens and pistil. A native of the

Hen-and-chickens (*Sempervivum tectorum*)

Hibiscus (*Hibiscus rose-sinensis*)

tropics, hibiscus should be brought indoors or into a greenhouse if winter temperatures frequently drop below 30°F. Rich, well-drained soil kept moist during the summer, plenty of sun, and monthly applications of fertilizer from April to September are necessary for them to flourish. During extreme summer temperatures (over 90°F), they should be provided with shade during the hottest part of the day. Pruning for shape is best done in the spring. There are many cultivars with differing growth rates or shapes and size or color of the blossoms. They grow to a height of 6 to 15 feet tall, depending on their cultural environment. The flowers are used to brew a tea, dried for color in potpourri, or boiled to produce a dye (successful only with dark-colored flowers).

Hollyhock/Marsh Mallow (*Alcea rosea/Althaea officinalis*)

Towering hollyhocks are among the most impressive planting in any garden. Spirelike flower spikes from 5 to 10 feet tall are covered with blooms in many shades of pink, red, yellow, or white. The plants are biennials but self-sow so freely that they are usually treated as perennials.

The look-alike marsh mallow is a perennial that has long been associated with herb gardening. Its flower spikes grow only to 4 feet with small bluish to pale rose flowers and gray velvety leaves. Both plants have been grown in the past for medicinal use. Today they are favorites for the flower border.

Plant both in full sunlight and well-drained soil. Marsh mallows prefer fairly wet soil. Spider mites are especially fond of these plants, so be on your guard and keep the malathion handy. Propagate by seeds or division.

Hollyhock (*Alcea rosea*)

Hops (*Humulus lupulus*)

This perennial vine is well suited in temperate regions as a screen or arbor plant. Shoots will often grow 25 to 30 feet in one season, producing a downy stem and dark green leaves. The cultivar 'Aureus' has yellow foliage. The summer-blooming female flower, a squat yellow catkin, is a prime ingredient in beer; the heavy—if not heady—aroma it emits may not be to everyone's liking. Plant hops in a sunny spot in rich loamy soil and give it lots of water. Propagate from root cuttings.

Horehound (*Marrubium vulgare*)

White velvety leaves and downy stems characterize this small half-hardy perennial that grows to 18 inches. Small white flowers that attract bees are produced along the stems in late summer. The leafy tops were used as a cough suppressant which is familiar to us now as a candy. Plant horehound in full sun and poor soil that remains on the dry side. Propagate by seeds or division.

Right: Hop (*Humulus lupulus*) catkins

Far right: Horehound (*Marrubium vulgare*)

Horseradish (*Armoracia rusticana*)

The pungent roots of horseradish are important additions to the culinary garden. The 15-inch tall plant has glossy green leaves and profuse small white flowers. It is a hardy perennial but is best treated as an annual.

To keep the plant from spreading as a weed and to assure quality roots, in the spring prepare a mound of soil 2 feet high by 2 feet wide and as long as you need. Cut the roots into 9-inch sections and plant them in the side of the mound, spaced 12 inches apart and 12 to 18 inches above normal ground level. Position them on a slant, small end down and large end 2 to 3 inches below the soil surface. Keep the soil moist throughout the growing season.

After the leaves get about 12 inches high, push back the soil above the cuttings and remove all but one or two of the crown sprouts. Rub off the small roots that have started from the sides of the cuttings but be sure not to disturb the branch roots at the base. Recover the root with soil. For particularly fine horseradish, repeat this operation in about 4 weeks. Delay harvest until October or November. Store roots in a cool dark place.

Horseradish (*Armoracia rusticana*)

Jasmine (*Jasminum* species)

Hyssop (*Hyssopus officinalis*)

This compact, shrubby perennial stays under 2 feet tall. Smooth, narrow, aromatic opposite leaves grow on woody stems with spikes of white, pink, or blue flowers. Hyssop can be trimmed like a boxwood hedge, but older plants may become too woody. A look-alike relative, the giant or anise hyssop (*Agastache foeniculum*) grows slightly larger. Use the leaves as a fragrance and the flowers for decoration.

Plant hyssop in full sun and well-drained, slightly alkaline soil. Propagate by seed, stem cuttings, or root division.

Indigo, False (*Baptisia tinctoria*)

A North American native, the leaves, stems, and seedpods of the wild indigo plant are used to produce a blue dye. A bushy, perennial, herbaceous plant that grows from 2 to 4 feet high, it requires only ordinary soil in full sun, and moderate amounts of water. The summer-blooming flowers are a bright yellow and are not used as a dye. Propagate by division or seeds.

Jasmine (*Jasminum* species)

Fragrant blossoms make these erect or climbing shrubs a delight to the herb and spice gardener. Most have small, shiny, dark green leaves. Flowers in yellow or white appear in clusters at axils or tips. Gather the flowers to add to your collection of fragrances.

Some of the fragrant species from which you can choose are: *J. sambac*, an evergreen climber whose flowers are used to flavor tea; *J. officinale*, a semi-evergreen vine whose flowers are even more fragrant; and *J. odoratissimum*, an evergreen shrub and probably the most fragrant of all the jasmine flowers.

Jasmines can be grown outdoors all year only in warm regions; in other climates they must be grown as container plants that can be given protection, or established as greenhouse plants. They like sun or partial shade in ordinary garden soil and have no particular cultivation requirements. Propagate from cuttings of ripened wood in the fall.

Johnny-Jump-Up (*Viola tricolor*)

Miniature pansy or heart's ease is a charming little plant to add to the herb garden. It is a self-seeding biennial that grows about 6 to 8 inches high. Leaves vary from feathery to heart-shaped on the same stem. The small pansylike flowers are purple, yellow, and white and bloom throughout spring and summer. The flowers can be candied or used as a source of fragrance.

Plant this little viola in full sun and any soil that is kept moist but never

Juniper (*Juniperus communis* 'Echiniformis')

Lady's mantle (*Alchemilla vulgaris*)

soggy. Propagate from seed, but do not expect blooms until the second year. If you are in a hurry, set out nursery transplants.

Juniper (*Juniperus communis*)

The utility of this species lies in the berries the plants produce. They can be used as a spice in cooking, as a fragrance, or to produce a brown dye. Junipers have long been used as ornamental shrubs or trees in gardens and there are many varieties with differing growth habits (prostrate, shrubby, trees) and colors of foliage (dark green, light green, gray-green, gold) from which to choose. They can be used as a hedge, border plantings, ground covers, or screens.

Junipers prefer sandy and loamy soil that is kept moist though well drained, but will still perform well in dry gravelly soil. Full sun is usually the rule, though partial shade is acceptable; in areas of very hot summers, partial shade will probably be beneficial. Germination from seeds can take years, and cuttings are difficult; nursery plants are the quickest and most foolproof method of increase.

Lady's Mantle (*Alchemilla vulgaris*)

An undemanding, low-growing (6 to 8 inches) perennial, lady's mantle is well suited for a rock garden or as an edging for borders. The dull green foliage gives off a slightly sweet odor when crushed. Clusters of small yellowish or greenish flowers bloom in the summer. The leaves are used to brew a slightly aromatic tea and are also used in cosmetics. Give it routine care in any well-drained garden soil in a sunny location. Propagate by seeds or division.

Lamb's Ears (*Stachys byzantina*)

The soft fuzzy foliage gives this plant its common name. Woolly hairs cover the 3- to 6-inch gray-green leaves. Thick flower stalks with whorls of small purple flowers appear early in the summer.

Once considered to have medicinal properties, lamb's ears make an effective ground cover that closely hugs the ground. To establish, plant about 12 to 15 inches apart in full or partial sun and well-drained soil. Every 2 or 3 years, divide root clumps to avoid overcrowding. Frost can make the leaves mushy; trim back affected foliage in the spring. Propagate slowly from seed or more efficiently from divisions.

Lamb's ears (*Stachys byzantina*)

Lavender (*Lavandula* species)

Long-time favorites in the perennial or herb garden, lavenders are small shrubs growing in rounded clumps from 1½ to 4 feet high. Fragrant blooms, a source of perfume, are lavender to deep purple in color. Leaves can be bright green to gray. English lavender (*L. angustifolia*) is the most widely grown species. Some of the cultivars available include: 'Alba', which has white flowers; 'Fragrance', which is highly scented; and 'Compacta', which grows to only 8 inches tall. French lavender (*L. dentata*) has bright green foliage and a longer blooming period.

When harvesting for your fragrance collection, strip blooms from the stalk just at the start of flowering. This is the time to gather flower stalks for drying also. Prune the plant after it blooms to keep it looking neat.

Lavender requires full sun and very fast-draining soil. Keep on the dry side. Propagate from seed or stem cuttings.

Leek (*Allium ampeloprasum*)

A hardy member of the onion family, the leek looks like a fattened green onion with much larger leaves and practically no swelling of the bulb. The flavor is much milder than that of the onion however.

Leeks need deep soil and plenty of water and fertilizer. They have a long growing season; planted in the spring, they are harvested in the fall. Plant them 4 to 6 inches apart in trenches 4 to 6 inches deep. Pile soil around the stems as they grow to produce the long white edible part. Since it is difficult to prevent gritty particles of soil from getting in between the leaves, wrap corrugated cardboard around the stems before earthing them up. Start leeks from seed or transplants.

Lemon Balm (*Melissa officinalis*)

This lemon-scented plant is a member of the mint family and spreads as vigorously. A perennial, also known as sweet balm, it has a profusion of green leaves that grow to a height of 2 to 3 feet. There are small clusters of inconspicuous white flowers in summer. The leaves may be used as a flavoring in cooking, to brew a tea, or as a fragrance in sachets or potpourris.

Lemon balm prefers full sun or partial shade and relatively poor soil that is kept dry. It may not flourish in regions with very hot summers. Propagate from seed, cuttings, or division.

Lemon Verbena (*Aloysia triphylla*)

The delightfully lemonlike fragrance of the leaves is sufficient reason to grow this tender shrub. Sometimes sold as *Lippia citriodora*, the plant grows to 10 feet in height. Plant low-growing perennials around it in the garden to soften its leggy appearance. Pale green leaves in groups of three or four are usually deciduous but sometimes evergreen. Clusters of small white or lilac flowers bloom in the summer. The leaves may be used as a culinary flavoring, to brew a refreshing tea, or added to your fragrance collection.

Give the plant full sun and routine garden care. It is successful as a container plant indoors or out. Provide winter protection to keep the plant evergreen. Propagate by cuttings of new growth.

Licorice (*Glycyrrhiza glabra*)

The crushed or ground roots of this perennial herb are boiled in water to yield the syrup which when hardened is the candy familiar to most children. Chips of the root or a powdered form are normally used in baking or other confections. Licorice can only be grown in mild regions in deeply prepared (to 2½ feet), moist, rich soil. The leaves, slightly sticky on the undersides, form a bushy mass 2 to 3 feet high, and clusters of small blue or violet flowers blossom in the spring and summer. The plant tolerates partial shade, but the soil should be kept evenly moist at all times.

Lavender (*Lavandula* species)

Leeks (*Allium ampeloprasum*)

Lemon balm (*Melissa officinalis*)

Lily-of-the-valley (*Convallaria majalis*)

Small-leaved European linden (*Tilia cordata*)

Lotus (*Nelumbo nucifera*)

Licorice spreads by runners along the ground, so keep these clipped back if you do not want your plants to spread. When commercially grown, roots are harvested after 3 or 4 years; you should probably let your plants grow at least 2 years before harvesting. Propagate from seed, root division, or the small plants produced by runners.

Lily-of-the-Valley (*Convallaria majalis*)

These charming plants will delight you every year in early spring with their nodding, sweetly fragrant, bell-like flowers posed against light green leaves. The blossoms will add to your collection of fragrances and the leaves may be used to produce a green dye. Lilies-of-the-valley are easily grown in moderately rich soil in a shady (at least partially shady), moist location. Plant pips (a vertical rootstalk that grows off the main horizontal root) obtained from a nursery or by mail order in November or December 1½ inches deep, in clusters for best effect. Top dress the planting area with a small amount of manure and mulch. The plants will then need no further care other than moisture when growing and an annual topdressing of fertilizer and mulch in the fall. After 4 or 5 years the bed will become too crowded, and the production of blooms will fall drastically. Dig up the bed, select new pips, and start over again.

If you live in an area with a mild winter climate, lilies-of-the-valley will not bloom well. A method of forcing them into bloom in these areas, as well as preparing potted plants that will bloom indoors, is as follows: store the pips in plastic bags in the vegetable compartment of your refrigerator from September until planting in November or December. If planted in a container for your enjoyment indoors, after the plant has bloomed, place the pot outside in a shady place and keep it well watered. In the fall repeat the process with new pips.

Linden (*Tilia* species)

The fragrant, summer-blooming flowers of the linden are a great attraction to bees as well as to the herbalist who may wish to collect them for a potpourri or use in cosmetics. Deciduous trees, lindens take cold winters well and will adapt to most soils, but are not drought tolerant. They grow tall (to 100 feet) in a pyramidal shape. The drooping clusters of yellowish white flowers contrast against the dark green leaves. Keep a vigilant eye out for aphids and spray as necessary. If the tree is sprayed while in bud or in bloom, do *not* use the flowers in cosmetics.

Lotus (*Nelumbo* species)

Every part of the beautiful lotus is edible—its tuberous roots, leaves, flowers, and seeds. The American lotus (*N. lutea*) has showy fragrant, pale yellow blooms and large (1 to 2 feet across) blue-green leaves that stand 2 feet above the water. The East Indian lotus (*N. nucifera*) is a larger species with white or pink flowers.

To grow from seed, slightly notch the seeds to facilitate germination. Plant in 6-inch pots of rich soil and add a top layer of clean sand. Submerge the pot 6 to 8 inches in a larger container filled with water. The top layer of sand in the pot will keep the water clear. Set the pots deeper in the container as the plants begin to grow so that there is at least 6 inches of water over the soil surface. Lotus is hardy in the north as long as the rootstalk does not freeze.

Lovage (*Levisticum officinale*)

A celery look-alike, lovage is a perennial that grows to heights of 3 to 7 feet. It bears greenish flowers in the summer. Lovage seeds and leaves taste and smell like celery, and they are used as a seasoning in much the same manner.

Grow in full sun or partial shade and rich soil that is kept evenly moist. Lovage dies back to the ground in winter and needs freezing temperatures.

It is difficult to grow in warm coastal areas. Propagate from just-ripened seed or root division in the spring.

Madder (*Rubia tinctorum*)

The root of this perennial herb is used to produce a red dye. A rather untidy plant, madder tends to sprawl if its height of 3 to 4 feet is not kept staked. Summer brings tiny yellow flowers on spikes between the rough-textured leaves and stems, followed by red berries that later turn black. Madder likes light sandy soil in full sun and regular, though not frequent, watering. It spreads by numerous underground runners but can be contained by sunken header boards. Propagate by seeds or root division.

Lovage (*Levisticum officinale*)

Malva (*Malva sylvestris*)

This hardy biennial is usually treated as an annual. Sow seeds in place in the garden in the spring. Plants grow from 2 to 3 feet tall with deeply cut, almost lacy, green leaves on rough hairy stems. The summer blooms are showy rose-purple flowers, with darker veins, up to an inch across. As well as being decorative in borders, dried malva flowers and leaves can be used to brew a delicately flavored tea, or the dried flowers can be used to add color to a potpourri. Plant in a sunny location in any well-drained soil. Propagate from seeds. The variety *mauritiana* grows taller on smooth stems and has darker-colored flowers.

Marjoram (*Origanum majorana*)

A perennial grown as an annual, marjoram reaches 1 to 2 feet in height. The small oval leaves are light green on top, gray-green underneath and covered with fine hairs. Flowers form in tight clusters of white to lilac, but the foliage should be harvested just before blooming. Marjoram is used primarily as a culinary seasoning. Its subtle fragrance combines well with other herbs.

Grow in full sun and slightly alkaline soil kept slightly moist. Propagate by seeds, cuttings, or layering.

Malva (*Malva sylvestris*)

Marsh Mallow *see* Hollyhock

Mint (*Mentha* species)

The mints are all fast-growing, fast-spreading perennials. Like common peppermint (*M.* × *piperita*), they all have square stems and opposite aromatic leaves.

The stiff stems of the apple mint (*M. suaveolens*) grow 20 to 30 inches. The variegated, rounded leaves are slightly hairy. Small purplish white flowers are produced on 2- to 3-inch spikes.

Peppermint (*M.* × *piperita*) grows from 1 to 2 feet, spreads rapidly, and produces small purple flowers on 1- to 3-inch spikes. Its strongly scented leaves are an enjoyable flavoring for tea.

Orange bergamot (*M.* × *piperita* var. *citrata*) has a similar growth habit, but the stems are reddish green, the oval leaves are often edged in purple, and light purple flowers bloom in the uppermost axils. The leaves have an orange odor when crushed.

Pennyroyal (*M. pulegium*) is characterized by small oval hairy leaves on creeping stems that grow to 2 feet in length. Lavender-blue or pink flowers grow in tiers on 6- to 12-inch-long flower spikes.

The mint jelly herb, spearmint (*M. spicata*), grows to a height of 1 to 2 feet with reddish stems and crinkly pointed leaves. Flower spikes of 2 to 4 inches are lavender in color.

All mints thrive in partial shade and moderately rich, moist soil. Keep roots under control with sunken header boards or plant in underground pots. Cut flowering stalks before they go to seed. Propagate by stem cuttings, root division, or layering.

Marjoram (*Origanum majorana*)

Orange bergamot (*Mentha* x *piperita* var. *citrata*)

Mustard (*Brassica nigra*)

If you wait too long to harvest the seeds of this hardy annual, it will spread throughout your garden and your spice crop will have turned into a weedy pest. For this reason you may wish to gather mustard seeds for cooking from wild-growing plants. Mustard likes heavy soil, moderate watering, and full sun in cool weather. Sow seeds in early spring or, in the fall in mild climates. The plants grow tall (2 to 3 feet) and rangey, with yellow flowers. Two other species, *B. hirta* and *B. juncea*, the latter of which is grown for edible greens, also produce pungent seeds.

Mustard (*Brassica nigra*)

Myrtle (*Myrtus communis*)

Cultivars of this highly aromatic evergreen shrub grow from 3 to 10 feet tall, or more under ideal conditions. Small shiny leaves, tiny fragrant flowers, and peppery berries characterize the plant. Myrtle is popular in formal gardens because it can be pruned to almost any form. Use the dried leaves as a fragrant addition to potpourris or sachets.

Grow in full sun or partial shade and well-drained soil. In frost-free climates myrtle can be grown outdoors all year, in other areas it must be a container plant and moved to a protected winter location. Propagate from seed, cuttings or half-ripened wood, or by layering.

Myrtle (*Myrtus communis* 'Compacta')

Nasturtium (*Tropaeolum* species)

The peppery-tasting flowers and leaves of this climbing annual make colorful additions to summer salads. The buds and seeds can be pickled as a substitute for capers. Flowers have spurs and appear in orange, yellow, red, creamy white, salmon, and deep mahogany.

Tropaeolum majus is the most widely grown species; *T. minus* differs from it only in that it is a dwarf and does not climb. *T. tuberosum* has an edible tuber.

Grow nasturtiums in full sun and well-drained soil. If the soil is too rich or you overfeed them, there will be lots of lush foliage but few flowers. Watch for aphids that seem to thrive on nasturtiums. Propagate from seed.

Nasturtiums will grow indoors in bright sunlight or under artificial lighting. Keep the temperature cool. Feed with half-strength houseplant fertilizer monthly if you want flowers.

Nasturtium (*Tropaeolum majus*)

Onions (*Allium cepa*)

Onions are indispensable in the culinary herb and spice garden. In addition to the edible bulb, they produce interesting spikes of flowers that are good for drying. Also see Leek (page 115) and Garlic (page 109).

Any variety of the standard onion can be a "green onion," or scallion, if harvested when the bulb is small. 'White Lisbon' is the cultivar most widely grown for this purpose. There are also several cultivars known as bunching onions that do not produce bulbs at all and are eaten only as green onions.

Fully developed onions are harvested when the tops begin to yellow and fall over. Then they are sun dried for a few days and may be stored in a cool, dry, well-ventilated place for months.

Varieties are classed as long-day and short-day crops according to the day length at the time of harvest and come in white, yellow, and red bulbs. For the pearly or pickling onions, plant the variety 'Eclipse' thickly in the spring and harvest when quite young.

Egyptian onions produce clusters of small red bulblets and hollow stalks.

Shallots, prized by gourmets for their subtle flavor, are multiplier onions that divide into clumps of small bulbs. They are harvested and dried just as standard onions are.

Grow onions in plenty of sunlight and well-drained, deeply prepared, rich soil. If your season is short, start with transplants instead of seeds or sets.

Onion (*Allium cepa*)

Oregano (*Origanum vulgare*)

This tender perennial is a close relative of sweet marjoram but has a sharper flavor. It grows into a bushy plant up to 2½ feet tall with broad oval leaves that are dark green. Flowers are a pale pink. Replace container-grown plants when they get woody.

Grow in full sun and well-drained soil kept slightly moist. Propagate from seed, cuttings, or root division.

Oregano (*Origanum vulgare*)

Orris (*Iris × germanica* var. *florentina*)

Orris is the sweet scented roots of the German or Florentine iris that have been valued by herbalists for many centuries. It is used both for its own scent and as a fixative for other perfumes. Swordlike leaves grow to 2 feet high with large white and violet flowers that are veined with blue and marked with yellow beards.

Irises require full sun and well-drained soil. Cut the spring-blooming flowers after fading to prevent seed formation that will weaken rhizome growth. The foliage will die back in the fall. Dig up the plants every few years after flowering, discard the older "woody" rhizomes at the center of the clump, and replant the actively growing terminal rhizomes. When planting, place the rhizomes horizontally just at the soil surface with the roots pointed down. Peel and dry rhizomes in the sun to be ground up for use in herbal fragrances.

Papaya (*Carica papaya*)

Besides its delicious fruit, the leaves of this tropical tree can be used as a skin-softening ingredient in soaps and cosmetics. The papaya likes tropical temperatures, though it can take an infrequent few degrees of frost. It needs a rich well-drained soil and lots of moisture to sustain its rapid growth to 25 feet high. Similar to palm trees in appearance, the plants are normally dioecious, meaning a plant bears either male or female flowers. Cultivars are now available that produce bisexual flowers. The papaya is fast growing and short lived, and it is most easily propagated from seed.

Orris (*Iris x germanica* var. *florentina*)

Paprika *see* Peppers

Parsley (*Petroselinum crispum*)

Parsley is a biennial but is usually grown as an annual. It has very dark green leaves that are deeply curled. The Italian variety *neapolitanum* has flat broad leaves. When harvesting, snip leaf stalks off at the base—do not pinch individual leaves—or the foliage will become tough. In cold regions parsley may be transplanted from the garden into a container before the first frost and brought inside to a sunny windowsill.

Parlsey prefers partial shade in moderately rich, moist soil. Propagate from seed. Parsley gets off to a slow start and is sometimes hard to germinate. Soak seed for 24 hours in warm water before planting or buy nursery transplants.

Passionflower (*Passiflora incarnata*)

A native of the southeastern United States, this perennial vine will die back at the first frost, but will vigorously begin climbing again the following spring. It will flourish in almost any kind of soil, and requires only a moderate amount of water in full sun. Be sure to give it something to grow on (such as a trellis or arbor), and you will be rewarded with white or lavender flowers 2 to 3 inches across and small, yellowish, edible fruits. The dried and cut leaves and flowers may be used to brew a mild tea. The vine will quickly spread from root runners and could become invasive if not planted in a container or restricted bed. Propagate from seeds or new plants produced by the runners.

Parsley (*Petroselinum crispum*)

Peppers (*Capsicum annuum*)

Pomegranate (*Punica granatum*)

Rocket (*Eruca vesicaria* subspecies *sativa*)

Pennyroyal *see* Mint

Peppers (*Capsicum annuum*)

The familiar green or red pepper is unrelated to the black and white pepper-corn spice of the Far East. You have a big choice in the degree of hotness to plant in the garden, from sweet mild peppers that are dried and ground into paprika to the hot jalapeno peppers. For chili choose from the following varieties: 'Red Chili', 'Long Red Cayenne', 'Hungarian Wax', and 'Chili Jalapeno'. All are hot and can be dried, then ground. The Tabasco pepper (*C. frutescens*) is rarely grown in gardens.

Peppers need hot weather to set fruit, but daytime temperatures over 90°F (32°C) will cause the flowers to drop, as will night temperatures much below 60°F (16°C).

Peppers are easiest to start as transplants from a nursery, or grow your own seedlings indoors. Do not transplant them into the garden until the weather is quite warm. Keep peppers well watered, especially at flowering time when you should also give them a light application of fertilizer.

Peppers make attractive container plants, especially pimientos or the small-fruited hot varieties. They do well indoors, even under lights. Out-doors, they add color to flower beds or herbaceous borders.

Pimiento *see* Peppers

Pomegranate (*Punica granatum*)

A small deciduous tree or shrub, the pomegranate will grace your garden with summertime orange-red flowers and in the autumn with brilliant yellow foliage and the round, purplish red fruit. Additionally, the bark may be used as a dark red dye, the seeds dried and used as a spice, and the dark red juice from the pulp surrounding the seeds as a coloring or slightly tart addition to drinks.

Pomegranates grow best in hot, arid, southern areas, but can be grown in the north in containers if given protection indoors during the winter. For successful production of fruit, deep watering during the summer months is necessary; otherwise moderate watering is sufficient. There are a number of cultivars (not all of which bear fruit) with different colored flowers ('Alba Plena', white) or double flowers ('Chico'), and also a dwarf form ('Nana') that serves well as a container plant or low hedge. Propagate by hardwood cuttings in the spring.

Rocket (*Eruca vesicaria* subspecies *sativa*)

This weedy annual is known to the French as *roquette*, the Greeks call it *roka*, and the Italians *arugula*. It's a low-growing plant that looks like mus-tard with white, yellow, or purple edible flowers. The young leaves have a horseradish flavor; use sparingly as a salad garnish.

Grow rocket in full sun. It is a cool-weather crop and becomes bitter during hot summers. New growth is the most tender, so keep the plant well trimmed to encourage growth. Propagate from seeds; you may start harvest-ing leaves about 2 months later.

Rosemary (*Rosmarinus officinalis*)

This old favorite is an evergreen shrub which is not quite winter hardy and grows between 2 and 4 feet in height. Except in mild winter climates it should be grown in movable containers so it can winter over in a cool, frost-free location. The leaves are needlelike, glossy green over gray-green and are used in cooking. Flowers are in clusters of lavender to blue and are used in perfume.

Grow in full sun and well-drained soil. Keep fairly dry. Propagate by seed or cuttings of half-ripened wood.

Rosemary (*Rosmarinus officinalis*, dwarf cultivar)

Roses (*Rosa* species)

If you have ever delighted in the aroma of one of the old roses, chances are you have already added one to your garden. The fragrances are heavy and lingering. Old roses are easy to grow, quite hardy, and pest free. They may have single or double flowers and come mostly in shades of pink, rose, and white, with a few yellows.

The scent of the foliage of the sweetbriers (*R. eglanteria*) is reminiscent of ripe apples. Damask roses (*R. damascena*) are the source of attar of roses used in perfumes. Moss roses (*R. centifolia* 'Muscosa') are covered with a soft mossy growth over the calyx and a stem that leaves a sticky, fragrant resin on your fingers.

Other roses to consider that blend well with herbs and provide fragrant petals for cooking and crafts include the apothecary's rose (*R. gallica*), the cabbage rose (*R. centifolia*), tea rose (*R. odorata*), hybrid perpetuals, noisettes (*R. × noisettiana*), and hybrid musks. *R. rugosa* is valued for its large hips, rich in vitamin C.

Plant roses in full sun in well-drained, rich soil. You cannot give roses too much water as long as the drainage is good. Unlike the modern roses, one feeding in the early spring is enough for most old species.

Older species may not be available at your neighborhood nursery. Roses may be propagated from softwood stem cuttings, so you may be able to obtain cuttings from a friend or a nearby botanical or rose garden. A number of nurseries that specialize in older roses issue mail-order catalogs.

Rose (*Rosa* species)

Safflower (*Carthamus tinctorius*)

Also known as false saffron, this annual grows from 1 to 2 feet high with spiny green leaves. The orange flowers resemble thistles. The tiny red florets and yellow styles are dried in separate piles to produce red and golden yellow powders, the latter sometimes used as a substitute for true saffron but more importantly used as a yellow dye. The seeds are the source of safflower oil.

Plant in light soil in a warm sunny location. Safflower grows best in dry summer climates without much rainfall. Propagated by seeds, which germinate easily.

Saffron (*Crocus sativus*)

You will have to grow a lot of flowers in order to gather enough golden saffron to use as a spice. But the little fall crocus blooms are so pretty you might want to have a large planting of them. Once you have harvested and dried all the tiny orange stigmas from the center of the crocus, you will understand the high price you have to pay for saffron.

Saffron crocus grows from a 1-inch corm. Stems are from 3 to 4 inches tall topped with a starlike lavender flower. The grasslike leaves appearing with the flower can reach 18 inches and stay green until spring.

Plant bulbs 3 to 4 inches deep late in summer in full sun (although they will tolerate a bit of shade) in a rich well-drained soil. The corms multiply naturally underground and you can propagate them by dividing the clumps every few years.

Sage (*Salvia* species)

The familiar garden sage (*S. officinalis*) is a hardy small shrub which grows to 2 feet tall. It has long oval, gray-green leaves that are coarsely textured. Violet-blue flowers appear on tall spikes. A dwarf variety looks the same except for size.

The cultivar 'Golden Sage' is characterized by yellow markings on the leaf edges. It grows as easily as the common form. The white and purple-red markings on the leaves make variegated sage ('Tricolor') showier than the species and desirable in many landscapes.

Sage (*Salvia* species)

Creeping St.-John's-wort (*Hypericum calycinum*)

Sassafras (*Sassafras albidum*)

Winter savory (*Satureja montana*)

Pineapple sage (*S. elegans*) is less hardy than *S. officinalis*. It grows to a height of 2 to 3 feet. Light green leaves are delightfully fruity in fragrance. Scarlet flowers occur in the fall. Requirements are the same as for other sages.

Chia (*S. columbariae*) is a low-growing (4 to 20 inches) sage with blue flowers. Collect the seeds in the fall and sprout them on a damp paper towel. The sprouts make a delightful, delicate-tasting addition to salads.

Sage needs full sun and grows best in poor, well-drained, somewhat dry soil. Propagate by seed, stem cuttings, or layering.

St.-John's-Wort (*Hypericum* species)

There are more than three hundred species of St.-John's-wort in a variety of forms, such as ground covers, evergreen and deciduous shrubs, or herbaceous perennials, but all are easily grown and share the distinctive yellow-petaled flower with numerous stamens. Most species are hardy enough to withstand all but the most extreme freezing temperatures. All prefer partial shade, moderate amounts of water, and good loamy soil. Propagate from seeds. The flowering tops are used to prepare a dye or a coloring for cosmetics.

A sampling of the species might include: *H. calycinum*, or creeping St.-John's-wort, a hardy, shrubby ground cover which performs best in shade; *H. perforatum*, a herbaceous perennial growing to 2 feet; and *H. hookeranum*, an evergreen shrub suited only to warm climates which grows 6 feet tall.

Santolina (*Santolina* species)

Almost indispensable to the gray garden, lavender cotton (*S. chamae-cyparissus*), growing to 2 feet, makes an attractive edging or border shrub. The narrow finely-divided leaves are silvery gray. Small round yellow flowers appear in summer. The faster-growing species *S. virens* has dark green leaves and yellow flowers. The aromatic dried leaves have been used for medicinal purposes in the past and as an insect repellant.

Grow santolina in full sun in any well-drained soil mixture kept fairly dry. The plants are tender and should be moved indoors or otherwise protected where winters are harsh. Propagate by stem cuttings or layering.

Sassafras (*Sassafras albidum*)

This deciduous tree, a native of the eastern United States, is often grown as an ornamental, reaching a height of more than 60 feet in a pyramidal shape. Small yellow flowers appear in the spring along with the light green leaves, followed by dark blue fruits on red stalks, with a grand finale in the autumn of orange-yellow and bright red leaves. The sassafras grows in almost any soil, requires only moderate water, and is hardy in the north (though it likes a warm and sunny location). Propagate from seeds, suckers, or root cuttings. The dried and powdered young leaves of the sassafras are the main ingredient in gumbo filé, and chips of the bark may be used as a scent in a potpourri. The roots are used to make sassafras tea.

Savory (*Satureja* species)

Perennial or winter savory (*S. montana*), produces weak stems to 15 inches and will stand temperatures down to 10°F (−12°C). Annual summer savory (*S. hortensis*) grows a little larger. It is more delicately flavored than the winter variety. Small narrow leaves grow in pairs along the stems and are used as a condiment. Flowers are small and pinkish white.

Both savories need full sun and well-drained soil. Annual (summer) savory prefers slightly rich soil, while the perennial (winter) species needs a sandy mix. Propagate annual savory from seed and perennial savory by division, layering, or cuttings of new growth.

Sesame (*Sesamum indicum*)

This tropical annual is grown for its nutty-tasting seeds. The plant grows to a height of 1 to 2 feet and has green leaves 3 to 5 inches long. There are 1-inch trumpet flowers in summer, white with pastel markings.

You will need many plants if you expect a quantity of seed as each plant can be harvested only once and produces about a tablespoon of seed.

Plant in full sun in any well-drained soil. Sesame needs 120 days of hot weather and routine garden care to produce seeds.

Shallot *see* Onion

Shisho (*Perilla frutescens* 'Crispa')

Giving off a cinnamonlike fragrance, the 3- to 6-inch long leaves of this annual are dark and covered with whitish hairs on top and purple hairs underneath. The plant grows 2 to 4 feet tall and produces small pinkish flower spikes. The seeds are a frequently used Oriental seasoning.

Plant shisho, also known as purple perilla (because of its burgundy stem) or summer coleus, in full sun or partial shade. Routine watering is sufficient. Keep the plant bushy and full by pinching the flower spikes as soon as they appear. Propagate by seeds.

Sorrel (*Rumex* species)

In this genus of perennials, garden sorrel (*R. acetosella*) has broad leaves and grows to about 3 feet; the leaves of French sorrel (*R. scutatus*) are narrower, darker, and grow close to the ground. The slightly acid-flavored leaves make a tangy addition to salads or cooked as a soup base. The flowering shoots, or dock, of French sorrel are popular in dried bouquets.

Grow in full sun and fairly moist, heavy soil. Propagate from seed or root division.

Southernwood *see* Artemisia

Speedwell (*Veronica officinalis*)

Popular as a ground cover, speedwell or St. Paul's betony is a creeping perennial with hairy stems and small oval, toothed leaves. Pale blue flower stalks grow from the leaf junctions. Use the leaves to brew a mildly flavored tea.

Speedwell will grow in almost any location (including full shade) in good soil that remains fairly dry. It is difficult, if not impossible, to grow in southern coastal regions. Propagate from seed, stem cuttings, or root divisions.

Star Anise (*Illicium verum*)

The common name of this evergreen tree derives from the star-shaped clusters of fruit that impart a flavor similar to that of anise. The fruit clusters are preceded by small round flowers appearing at first whitish, and then turning to pink and purple. The fruit should be picked before it has ripened for use as a culinary spice, and chips of the bark may be used to provide fragrance to potpourri or burned with charcoal as an incense. A slow grower that can reach a height of 60 feet, star anise can only be grown in warm climates. Propagate by seed or half-ripened cuttings.

Strawberry (*Fragaria vesca*)

Producing rather smaller plants and fruits than the "garden strawberry" usually grown for fruit, this species, commonly known as the woodland strawberry, will prove decorative in your garden or in a container as well as provide you with fresh leaves for brewing a mildly strawberry-flavored tea. The fruit is less sweet and juicy than the garden variety, but nonetheless

Sesame (*Sesamum indicum*)

Shisho (*Perilla frutescens* 'Crispa')

Sorrel (*Rumex* species)

Speedwell (*Veronica officinalis*)

Woodland strawberry (*Fragaria vesca*)

Sumac (*Rhus glabra*)

Sunflower (*Helianthus annuus*)

Sweet cicely (*Myrrhis odorata*)

tasty and refreshing. Strawberries like rich, moisture-retentive but well-draining soil with a moderate amount of water. Unlike its garden relatives, the woodland strawberry does well in partial shade. In northern areas, cover the plants with a straw mulch after the first couple of frosts. All strawberries produce well for 3 or 4 years, but should then be replaced by the new plants formed at the ends of runners.

Sumac (*Rhus glabra*)

An easily grown deciduous shrub or small tree, sumac will provide you with a display of green foliage and plumes of green flowers in the summer, followed in the autumn by scarlet foliage and dense heads of dark red berries. The leaves, berries, and roots may be used to prepare a dark red dye and the autumn foliage may be used as a handsome accent in arrangements. Sumac will grow in any garden soil in a sunny location, requires little water, and is unaffected by frost. Propagate from seeds or root cuttings.

Sunflower (*Helianthus annuus*)

These giant annuals will provide a tall (to 10 feet) dramatic background in your garden. The seeds may be used as a spice or roasted as a snack, and the orange-yellow petals around the circumference of the flower may be used to prepare a yellow dye. Sunflowers grow in any garden soil in full sun and need only a moderate amount of water. In regions with a short growing season, start seeds indoors in March.

Sweet Cicely (*Myrrhis odorata*)

All parts of this ancient herb smell and taste like anise. It is a perennial that grows 2 to 3 feet in height with fernlike foliage that is downy on the underside. The hollow stems bear small clusters of tiny white flowers in late spring, followed by shiny black seeds.

Plant sweet cicely in partial shade in acid soil. Keep it moist. The edible taproot (delicious sliced in salads) grows deep, so the bed should be prepared to accommodate it. If you leave a few seeds, the plant will self-seed. Or propagate from cuttings of the taproot, making sure that each section contains an eye. The plant is easy to grow everywhere except in areas with warm winters since it requires cold weather.

Sweet Flag (*Acorus calamus*)

The lemon-scented leaves and sweet-smelling rhizomes make this hardy perennial bog plant desirable to the herb gardener. Clumps of tall swordlike leaves grow to 2 feet or more. A cylindrical flower spike studded with minute greenish yellow flowers grows at an angle from the stem. In addition to the fragrance provided by the leaves in the garden, the dried root may be added to potpourris or sachets.

The plant will grow best along the edges of a water garden but can be raised in rich garden soil that is kept wet. In either case, it should be in full sun. Propagate by root division.

Sweet Olive (*Osmanthus fragrans*)

If you want to make a potpourri or create your own fragrances, you will certainly want to add the flowers of this evergreen shrub to the garden. In the garden it can reach a height of about 10 feet. As a container-grown plant it stays much smaller, under 3 feet indoors. Tiny white flowers in late winter and spring are highly fragrant and reminiscent of old New Orleans where it grows profusely. Leaves are finely toothed and glossy green.

Sweet olive grows best in partial shade where it can be protected from wind. Put in bright indirect light indoors. Almost any well-draining soil will do as long as it stays slightly moist. In colder climates, it should be protected from frosts.

Tansy (*Tanacetum vulgare*)

The bright green leaves of this hardy perennial are large and fernlike. Plants grow to 3 feet tall. Flat terminal clusters of buttonlike golden yellow flowers bloom late in the summer. The variety *crispum* produces more luxuriant and lacier foliage. The dried aromatic leaves and colorful flowers may be used in potpourris, the dried young leaves are a soothing ingredient in bath sachets, the root may be used to produce a green dye, and the foliage and flowers are attractive in freshly cut arrangements. Clusters of the flowers may also be dried for winter bouquets.

Tansy requires full sun, but will adapt to any soil that is not too wet. Propagate from seed or divisions; thin clumps every couple of years.

Sweet olive (*Osmanthus fragrans*)

Tarragon (*Artemisia dracunculus*)

French tarragon is a perennial that spreads by rhizomes. When fully grown (3 to 5 feet), it makes a graceful plant. It has slender dark green leaves and greenish flowers bloom in small clusters. The leaves provide the sweet-flavored herb used in cooking.

Grow in full sun or partial shade and well-drained soil. Protect plants with mulch in harsh winter climates. Propagate by division or root cuttings.

Tansy (*Tanacetum vulgare*)

Tea (*Camellia sinensis*)

Because of the intricate processing necessary to produce the dried herb we know as tea from the young leaves of this plant, growing your own tea is not really practical. You will find, though, that this evergreen shrub, which can grow to 15 feet tall, will make an attractive ornamental in subtropical regions or grown in a container in a greenhouse. Like other camellias, the tea plant enjoys well-drained, slightly acid soil in partial shade. Keep the soil moist during the hot summer months and fertilize during the spring. The glossy, dark green leaves are a perfect foil for the white nodding flowers in the summer. Propagate from cuttings of new growth.

Thyme (*Thymus* species)

All the members of this genus of aromatic perennials have woody twiglike stems and tiny, highly scented leaves. Common or garden thyme (*T. vulgaris*) is a low shrub (to 15 inches) useful as a border or edging plant or in a container. The subdued green of the foliage is complemented in the summer by white or varying shades of lilac flowers. Lemon thyme (*T. × citriodorus*) is similar in appearance though with shinier lemon-scented leaves. Both species have cultivars 'Argentus' and 'Aureus' which provide silver-colored and gold-trimmed foliage respectively. Keep both of these shrubs well trimmed to prevent them from becoming woody.

Two ground cover thymes are also of interest to the herb gardener: wild thyme (*T. serpyllum*), which forms a thick mat of foliage with purple flowers, and caraway thyme (*H. herba-barona*), which grows similarly, but has rose-colored flowers and leaves with the scent of caraway. Both these ground covers should be protected from protracted freezing weather or snow by a mulch.

Tarragon (*Artemisia dracunculus*)

Thyme (*Thymus* species)

Besides using these thymes as culinary herbs, or to add fragrance to cosmetics, sachets, or potpourris, lemon thyme can be used to brew a most refreshing tea. All thymes require light, well-drained soil that is kept fairly dry in full sun. Propagate by cuttings or division.

Turmeric (*Curcuma domestica*)

This perennial herb, grown for its tuberous rhizomes, is adaptable only to warm climates or greenhouse culture. When dried and powdered the rhizomes yield a spice similar to ginger used in curries and as a yellow dye. Turmeric grows in full sun in a rich, well-drained soil. Large long leaves are produced in the spring, followed by 2- to 3-foot high flower spikes with large white bracts and pale yellow flowers; the whole plant dies back in the fall. Keep moist during the growing season. Propagate by division of rhizomes in the spring.

Valerian (*Valeriana officinalis*)

A long-time favorite in herb gardens, this herbaceous perennial will be a colorful addition to your garden. From a mass of green foliage close to the ground, the stems rise to about 3½ feet with clusters of white, pink, or lavender flowers. (The cultivars 'Alba' and 'Rubra' have white and red flowers respectively.) The stems, leaves, and flowers have a heavy spice fragrance that not everyone finds to their liking. Valerian grows in just about any soil and needs only moderate water and full sun. The plant spreads easily with root suckers; propagate by division of these or by seeds. The dried and chopped roots are used in bath sachets.

Vanilla (*Vanilla planifolia*)

Grown mostly in Mexico and Madagascar, this vinelike climbing orchid is valued for the seed pod or bean, the source of vanilla. Your plant will probably not bear any beans to use as a flavoring, but it is ornamental in a warm greenhouse.

The rampant vine has 8-inch leaves along the fleshy stems. One cultivar is variegated. Mature plants produce 3-inch yellowish flowers. Artificial pollination is necessary to produce the beanlike pods, which must undergo a complex fermentation process before the characteristic flavor is developed.

Provide the vanilla orchid with supports on which to climb. Pot in osmunda fiber or rich humus orchid compost. The plant thrives with lots of water and high humidity and needs shade. Propagate by stem cuttings.

Vervain (*Verbena canadensis*)

A perennial usually grown as an annual in the north, this species is low-growing to a maximum height of 18 inches and is often used as a ground cover under tall perennials. Spikes of small lilac flowers appear in the spring or summer. Vervain is adaptable to most garden soils in full sun and should be kept moist during the summer. Propagate from seeds or make cuttings from new growth in the spring. The cultivar 'Rosea' has a long blooming period with rose-purple fragrant flowers. The leaves are used to brew a strongly flavored tea.

Other species of interest are *V. officinalis* and *V. hastata*, both of which grow somewhat taller and produce violet and blue flowers respectively.

Violet (*Viola odorata*)

The deliciously sweet scent of violets is well known to connoisseurs of herbal fragrances. This perennial spreads from creeping shoots and forms an attractive ground cover of heart-shaped leaves with crinkled edges. The heavily scented flowers in deep violet, pink, or white appear in late spring.

Violets are native to wooded areas and should be planted in partial shade and fairly rich soil that is kept evenly moist. Protect them from freezing temperatures by a leaf mulch or a layer of evergreen boughs. Propagate from rooted offshoots or root division.

Water Chestnut (*Eleocharis dulcis*)

You don't need a water garden to grow this attractive aquatic rush plant—just a large tub of water will do. In the spring, half fill a container with ordinary topsoil and mix in a tablespoon of granular slow-release fertilizer. Add topsoil to within about 3 inches of the top and plant the water chestnut corms ½ inch below the soil surface. (Corms are available from supplies of aquatic plants.) Submerge the pot in a container of water or a shallow pool so that its soil surface stays from ½ to 2 inches below the surface of the water.

Valerian (*Valeriana officinalis*)

Sweet violet (*Viola odorata*)

Watercress (*Nasturtium officinale*)

The plant will produce rushlike brown stems 3 feet tall. When the foliage dies down in the autumn, tap the entire plant out of the pot. Wash the soil from the root mass with a hose and gather the small brown corms.

Watercress (*Nasturtium officinale*)

A gourmet's delight, this creeping perennial will grow submerged, floating, or in shallow moving water. Its stems with many branches reach 2 feet or more with dark green leaves composed of 3 to 11 leaflets. In early summer there are clusters of small white flowers at the stem ends.

The peppery-tasting herb grows wild in streams throughout the United States. To adapt it to home gardening, set plants or scatter seed on the edge of a moving stream or irrigation ditch. It grows easily. In lieu of a stream, you can grow watercress in a very rich, very moist garden soil. It will not be as prolific, but it will grow. Propagate from seed or stem cuttings, even those you purchase from a grocery store.

Witch Hazel (*Hamamelis virginiana*)

You may not wish to go to the trouble of distilling the bark and leaves of this deciduous shrub for the astringent they produce, but they may still be used in a bath sachet. The plant also has the advantage of blooming in the fall and winter when few other plants are in flower. *H. virginiana* produces straggly golden yellow flowers in the fall, often in concert with the bright yellow autumn foliage. Another species, *H. vernalias* blooms in winter or early spring. Witch hazel prefers moist soil of sand and peat in a sunny location, but will also do well in partial shade. Propagate from seeds, which take 2 years to germinate.

Witch hazel (*Hamamelis virginiana*)

Wood Betony (*Stachys officinalis*)

This perennial herb grows from a rosette of scalloped, heavily veined leaves. Dense flower spikes growing to 3 feet tall produce red-purple flowers in the spring. (The cultivar 'Alba' produces white flowers.) Betony prefers moist soil in partial shade. Propagate from seeds or division. The leaves may be used to brew a mint-flavored tea and the flowers, either freshly cut or dried, make striking arrangements.

Wood betony (*Stachys officinalis*)

Woodruff (*Galium odoratum*)

The fragrance of woodruff (often called sweet woodruff) is not noticeable until the leaves are dried and crushed. A perennial that never reaches more than 14 inches in height, its dark green, pointed leaves grow in whorls around the stems. Plants produce profusions of tiny white, starlike summer flowers.

Use the dried leaves of woodruff as a culinary flavoring, to brew a sweet tea, or as a fragrance. It is one of the few herbs that grows well in full shade, but can take partial early morning or late afternoon sun. Grow in moist rich soil; do not let it dry out. Propagate by root division. Plants spaced a foot apart will soon form a thick mat of foliage.

Woodruff (*Galium odoratum*)

Wormwood *see* Artemisia

Yarrow (*Achillea millefolium*)

The hardy yarrows produce flat-headed flowers in yellow, white, or shades of red. The gray-green fernlike foliage grows to a height of 3 feet, though usually under 1 foot. Cut the flower stems back after the first (spring) flowering for a second round of blooms in the summer and fall.

Use the cut and dried leaves in a steam facial or as an astringent; the individual flowers may be used to prepare a dye; or the flowerheads, complete with stem, may be dried for arrangements. Grow yarrow in full sun and well-drained soil kept fairly dry. Propagate by division.

Yarrow (*Achillea millefolium*)

COMMERCIAL HERBS AND SPICES

Bee bread is another name for borage, and dittany of Crete is used for tea. Discover these and other facts in this listing of commonly sold herbs and spices.

On the following pages are herbs and spices with univeral appeal that are available in some preserved form from commerical suppliers. The many other herbs that are available that are not included here are generally used in medicines and home remedies.

Many of these plants can be grown and preserved at home—note the recommendations under *Home garden* in the notes accompanying each picture. In some cases, only certain regions or climates will prove hospitable to a plant. Other herbs can be grown anywhere but are not recommended for home cultivation because of their weedy appearance and wild growth habits. The cultural requirements for the herbs and spices suitable for the home garden are discussed in the Plant Selection Guide, beginning on page 96.

"Indoors/outdoors" means that the plants can be grown in either environment or can be rotated with the seasons. Plants recommended for indoors can be grown under artificial lighting. Some plants that are able to grow in a home garden will never produce a very large crop of the useful portion. These are suggested as ornamentals only.

Both common and botanical names are given. Some plants go by several common names and the first listing is the one judged to be most widely known. The nomenclature and spelling of botanical names are in agreement with *Hortus Third*, the recognized authority in horticulture.

A few botanical names have been reassigned or plants have been reclassified in the latest edition of *Hortus*, so you may find a few names that appear to be wrong if you compare them with names used by older guides. The reason for using the newest botanical identity is to help you when you want to locate a particular plant. Common names vary from region to region but the language of botany and horticulture remains consistent, if not constant.

As you read through the list you will see some words used repeatedly in plant names, a result of the original usage of the plant. For example, *officinalis* or *officinale* means that the plant was used for medicinal purposes at the time it was named. Likewise, *tinctoria* indicates that the plant was mainly used as a dye, and *odorata* suggests a sweet-smelling plant. Even though a plant's use has changed, the name remains the same.

In the listing, *Origin* tells you the region or regions to which the plant is native. *Parts* refers to the portion of the plant used: roots, stems, bark, leaves, flowers, or seeds. *Form* describes how the parts are used: whole seeds or cut leaves, for example.

Flavor or *Scent* refers to the taste or aroma of the useful plant part. In many cases the unique flavor or scent of an herb or spice has itself become a description, such as licorice, garlic, or vanilla.

Under *Uses* there is a brief note of the main ways that the plant's parts are used: culinary, cosmetics, or fragrance.

Mail-order sources for seeds and plants are listed on page 142.

ROSE LEAVES

CALAMUS

P. EX. GLYCYRR.

CITRUS AURANT. FLORA

CHELONE

P. SANTAL.

wood

AC. GALLIC.

Hydrastis Radix

Bergamot

P. CATECHU

RYOPHYL.

Agrimony
Church steeples,
cocklebur
Agrimonia eupatoria
Origin: Europe, North
Africa, Western Asia
Parts: Leaves, flowers
Scent: Apricot
Form: Cut
Uses: Dye, fragrance
Home garden: Outdoors

Alfalfa
Medicago sativa
Origin: Southwest Asia
Parts: Sprouted seeds,
leaves
Flavor: Delicate
Form: Whole seed, cut
leaves
Uses: Culinary, tea
(leaves)
Home garden: Not
recommended

Alkanet
Bugloss
Anchusa officinalis
Origin: Europe, Asia
Minor
Parts: Rootbark
Form: Pieces
Uses: Dye, furniture
stain
Home garden: Outdoors

Allspice
Pimenta dioica
Origin: West Indies,
Latin America
Parts: Berries
Flavor: Pungent
Form: Whole, ground
Uses: Culinary
Home garden: Not
recommended

Aloe vera
Aloe barbadensis
Origin: Dutch Antilles
Parts: Fleshy leaves
Flavor: Bitter
Form: Resin
Uses: Skin care
Home garden:
Indoors/outdoors,
container

Angelica
Archangel
Angelica species
Origin: Europe, Asia
Parts: Stalks, seeds,
roots
Flavor: Bitter
Form: Pieces and seed,
candied stalk
Uses: Culinary, tea
Home garden: Outdoors

Anise
Pimpinella anisum
Origin: Greece, Middle
East
Parts: Seeds
Flavor: Sweet, licorice
Form: Whole, candied
Uses: Culinary, liqueur,
cosmetics
Home garden:
Outdoors, difficult in
north

Annatto
Bixa orellana
Origin: Florida
Parts: Arils of seeds
Form: Whole
Uses: Dye, food
coloring
Home garden: Not
recommended

Arrowroot
Maranta arundinacea
Origin: West Indies
Parts: Rhizomes
Flavor: Tasteless
Form: Powdered
Uses: Culinary
Home garden: Indoors
as ornamental

Asparagus
Asparagus officinalis
Origin: Europe, North
Africa, Asia
Parts: Seeds, roots
Form: Whole seed, cut
root
Uses: Coffee substitute
(seed), tea (root)
Home garden: Outdoors

Barberry
Jaundice berry
Berberis vulgaris
Origin: Europe
Parts: Roots
Form: Cut
Uses: Dye
Home garden: Outdoors

Basil
Ocimum basilicum
Origin: Tropical Africa
Parts: Leaves
Flavor: Sweet
Form: Cut
Uses: Culinary
Home garden:
Indoors/outdoors

Bay
Laurus nobilis
Origin: Mediterranean
Parts: Leaves
Flavor: Sweet, spicy
Form: Whole, crushed
Uses: Culinary, fragrance
Home garden:
Indoors/outdoors
California bay
(*Umbellularia
californica*) often
substituted

Bayberry
Myrica pensylvanica
Origin: North America
Parts: Rootbark
Scent: Evergreen
Form: Cut
Uses: Candlemaking,
fragrance
Home garden: Outdoors

Bergamot, wild
Horsemint
Monarda punctata
Origin: North America
Parts: Leaves
Flavor: Minty
Form: Cut
Uses: Tea, fragrance
Home garden: Outdoors

Birch
Betula species
Origin: Northern Hemisphere
Parts: Bark, leaves
Form: Cut
Uses: Tea
Home garden: Outdoors

Blackberry
Rubus species
Origin: North America
Parts: Leaves, roots
Flavor: Mild
Form: Cut
Uses: Tea, dye
Home garden: Outdoors

Bloodroot
Sanguinaria canadensis
Origin: North America
Parts: Root
Form: Cut, ground
Uses: Dye
Home garden: Outdoors

Boneset
Eupatorium perfoliatum
Origin: North America
Parts: Leaves
Flavor: Bitter
Form: Crushed
Uses: Tea
Home garden: Outdoors

Borage
Bee bread, talewort, cool-tankard
Borago officinalis
Origin: Europe, North Africa
Parts: Leaves, stems, flowers
Flavor: Cucumber
Form: Cut
Uses: Culinary, tea
Home garden: Indoors/outdoors

Burdock
Beggar's buttons, cuckold, gobo, harlock
Arctium lappa
Origin: Eurasia, North America
Parts: Roots
Flavor: Mild
Form: Cut, powdered
Uses: Culinary
Home garden: Outdoors

Calendula
Marigold, pot marigold
Calendula officinalis
Origin: Southern Europe
Parts: Flowers
Flavor: Mild
Form: Petals
Uses: Culinary
Home garden: Indoors/outdoors

Capers
Capparis spinosa
Origin: Mediterranean
Parts: Flower buds
Flavor: Pungent
Form: Pickled
Uses: Culinary
Home garden: Outdoors, grow as annual in cold regions

Caraway
Carum carvi
Origin: Europe, North America
Parts: Seeds
Flavor: Licorice
Form: Whole
Uses: Culinary
Home garden: Outdoors except along coasts

Cardamom
Elettaria cardamomum
Origin: India
Parts: Seeds
Flavor: Spicy, pungent
Form: Whole, shelled, ground (green or roasted)
Uses: Culinary, fragrance
Home garden: Not recommended

Carob
Ceratonia siliqua
Origin: Eastern Mediterranean
Parts: Seeds, fruits
Flavor: Chocolatelike
Form: Cut, powdered (raw or roasted)
Uses: Culinary
Home garden: Outdoors, not in frost areas

Catnip
Catmint
Nepeta cataria
Origin: Eurasia
Parts: Leaves
Flavor: Sweet, minty
Form: Crushed
Uses: Tea, cat toys
Home garden: Indoors/outdoors

Cayenne
Capsicum annuum
Origin: North and South America
Parts: Podlike berries
Flavor: Hot
Form: Whole, ground
Uses: Culinary
Home garden: Outdoors

Cedar, red
Juniperus virginiana
Origin: North America
Parts: Wood
Scent: Evergreen
Form: Powdered, chips
Uses: Fragrance
Home garden: Outdoors

Celery
Apium graveolens
Origin: Worldwide
Parts: Seeds
Flavor: Mild
Form: Whole, ground
Uses: Culinary
Home garden: Outdoors

Chamomile
Camomile

Chamaemelum nobile
(Roman), *Matricaria
recutita* (German)

Origin: Western Europe,
Azores, North Africa

Parts: Flowers

Flavor: Applelike

Form: Whole

Uses: Tea, cosmetics,
fragrance

Home garden: Outdoors

Chervil
Anthriscus cerefolium

Origin: Europe, Western
Asia

Parts: Leaves

Flavor: Anise-parsley

Form: Crushed

Uses: Culinary

Home garden:
Indoors/outdoors

Chia
Salvia columbariae

Origin: Southwest
United States

Parts: Sprouted seeds

Flavor: Delicate

Form: Whole

Uses: Culinary

Home garden: Indoors

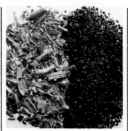

Chicory
Cichorium intybus

Origin: North Africa,
Europe, Western Asia

Parts: Roots

Flavor: Slightly bitter

Form: Raw or roasted

Uses: Coffee additive
or substitute

Home garden: Outdoors

Chili pepper
Capsicum annuum

Origin: North and South
America

Parts: Podlike berries

Flavor: Hot, spicy

Form: Whole, crushed,
ground

Uses: Culinary

Home garden: Outdoors

Chili powder
A mixture of ground chili
peppers with herbs and
spices

Chinese cinnamon
Cassia bark

Cinnamomum cassia

Origin: Burma, China,
Indonesia

Parts: Bark

Flavor: Sweet, spicy

Form: Pieces, ground

Uses: Culinary,
fragrance

Home garden: Not
recommended

Chinese five
spices
A mixture of ground star
anise, fennel, cinnamon,
cloves, and Szechwan
pepper.

Chives
Allium schoenoprasum

Origin: Europe, Asia

Parts: Leaves

Flavor: Mild

Form: Chopped

Uses: Culinary

Home garden:
Indoors/outdoors

Chocolate
Cocoa

Theobroma cacao

Origin: Central and
South America

Parts: Seeds

Flavor: Bitter

Form: Roasted, then
powdered or formed
into cakes

Uses: Culinary,
beverage

Home garden: Not
recommended

Chrysanthemum
Garland chrysanthe-
mum, crown daisy

*Chrysanthemum
coronarium*

Origin: Mediterranean

Parts: Young leaves,
flowers

Flavor: Mildly pungent

Form: Whole, petals

Uses: Culinary, garnish

Home garden: Outdoors

Cinnamon
Ceylon cinnamon

*Cinnamomum
zeylanicum*

Origin: Ceylon, India

Parts: Bark

Flavor: Sweet, pungent

Form: Pieces, ground

Uses: Culinary,
fragrance

Home garden: Not
recommended

Citrus
Citrus species

Origin: Asia

Parts: Fruit, flowers

Flavor: Sweet, acidic

Form: Diced or ground
peel, petals

Uses: Culinary,
fragrance, tea

Home garden:
Indoors/outdoors in
warm climates

Cloves
Syzygium aromaticum

Origin: Moluccas
(Indonesia)

Parts: Flower buds

Flavor: Pungent, sweet

Form: Whole, ground

Uses: Culinary,
fragrance

Home garden: Not
recommended

Coffee
Coffea arabica

Origin: Tropical Africa,
Latin America

Parts: Seeds

Flavor: Unique, slightly
bitter

Form: Roasted whole,
ground

Uses: Beverage,
culinary

Home garden: Indoors
or greenhouse as
ornamental

Cola nut

Cola acuminata
Origin: Tropical Africa
Parts: Seeds
Flavor: Cola
Form: Pieces, powdered
Uses: Beverage
Home garden: Not recommended

Coltsfoot

Tussilago farfara
Origin: Europe, west and north Asia, North Africa
Parts: Leaves
Flavor: Strong
Form: Cut
Uses: Dye, tea, tobacco substitute
Home garden: Not recommended

Comfrey

Blackwort, knit-bone
Symphytum officinale
Origin: Asia, Europe
Parts: Leaves, root
Flavor: Subtle
Form: Cut root, cut or powdered leaves
Uses: Tea
Home garden: Outdoors

Coriander

Cilantro, Chinese parsley
Coriandrum sativum
Origin: Southern Europe
Parts: Seeds (coriander), leaves (cilantro or Chinese parsley)
Flavor: Sweet, pungent
Form: Leaves cut; seed whole, ground
Uses: Culinary
Home garden: Indoors/outdoors

Cornflower

Bachelor's-button
Centaurea cyanus
Origin: Europe, Near East
Parts: Flowers
Form: Cut
Uses: Dye
Home garden: Outdoors

Cubeb

Piper cubeba
Origin: Southeast Asia
Parts: Berries
Flavor: Peppery
Form: Whole
Uses: Culinary
Home garden: Not recommended

Cumin

Cuminum cyminum
Origin: Mediterranean
Parts: Seeds
Flavor: Pungent, carawaylike
Form: Whole, ground
Uses: Culinary
Home garden: Outdoors in warm climates

Curry powder

A mixture of spices, such as fenugreek, turmeric, cumin, mustard seed, cardamom, ginger, and peppers ranging from mild to hot, used as seasoning

Damiana

Turnera aphrodisiaca
Origin: Tropical America
Parts: Leaves
Form: Cut
Uses: Tea
Home garden: Not recommended

Dandelion

Taraxacum officinale
Origin: Europe, Asia
Parts: Roots, leaves
Flavor: Slightly bitter
Form: Cut leaves, raw or roasted root pieces
Uses: Tea, coffee additive
Home garden: Outdoors if controlled

Desert tea

Mormon tea
Ephedra species
Origin: Northern Hemisphere
Parts: Leaves
Form: Cut
Uses: Tea
Home garden: Not recommended

Dill

Anethum graveolens
Origin: Southwest Asia
Parts: Leaves, seeds
Flavor: Sweet (leaves), slightly bitter (seeds)
Form: Seeds whole, leaves cut
Uses: Culinary
Home garden: Indoors/outdoors

Dittany of Crete

Hop marjoram
Origanum dictamnus
Origin: Greece
Parts: Flowers
Flavor: Marjoramlike
Form: Crushed
Uses: Tea
Home garden: Indoors/outdoors

Dyer's broom

Dyer's greenwood
Genista tinctoria
Origin: Europe, West Africa
Parts: Flowers and tops
Form: Cut
Uses: Dye
Home garden: Outdoors

Elderberry

Sambucus canadensis
Origin: North America
Parts: Flowers, berries, leaves
Flavor: Subtle
Form: Cut leaves and flowers, whole berries
Uses: Culinary, cosmetics, tea
Home garden: Outdoors

Elecampane

Inula helenium
Origin: Central America
Parts: Roots
Flavor: Bitter
Form: Cut
Uses: Liqueur flavoring, dye
Home garden: Outdoors

Eucalyptus

Gum tree
Eucalyptus species
Origin: Australia
Parts: Leaves
Scent: Menthol
Form: Whole or cut leaves
Uses: Fragrance, decoration
Home garden: Outdoors in mild climates

Fennel

Sweet fennel
Foeniculum vulgare
Origin: Southern Europe
Parts: Leaves, seeds
Flavor: Aniselike
Form: Seed whole or powdered, leaves cut
Uses: Culinary
Home garden: Outdoors

Fenugreek

Trigonella foenum-graecum
Origin: Southern Europe, Asia
Parts: Seeds
Flavor: Slightly bitter, maplelike
Form: Whole
Uses: Culinary, dye
Home garden: Outdoors

Filé

A mixture consisting chiefly of ground leaves of *Sassafras albidum* with other herbs and spices; used as a thickener in Creole cookery

Frankincense

Boswellia species
Origin: Asia, Africa
Parts: Resin
Scent: Sweet, spicy
Form: Gum
Uses: Fragrance
Home garden: Not recommended

Fumitory

Earth smoke
Fumaria officinalis
Origin: Northern temperate regions
Parts: Flowering foliage
Form: Cut
Uses: Dye
Home garden: Not recommended

Garam masala

A mixture of Indian spices, more fragrant and slightly sweeter than curry powder. It does not contain turmeric that gives yellow color to curries.

Garlic

Allium sativum
Origin: Northern Hemisphere
Parts: Bulb
Flavor: Strong, unique
Form: Whole, chips, powdered, juice
Uses: Culinary
Home garden: Outdoors

Germander

Teucrium chamaedrys
Origin: Europe, Southeast Asia
Parts: Leaves
Flavor: Mild
Form: Cut
Uses: Tea
Home garden: Outdoors

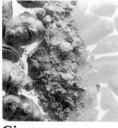

Ginger

Zingiber officinale
Origin: Southeast Asia
Parts: Rhizomes
Flavor: Strong, unique
Form: Whole, cut, ground, crystalized
Uses: Culinary
Home garden: Indoors/outdoors

Ginseng

Panax quinquefolius
Origin: North America, Eastern Asia
Parts: Roots, leaves
Flavor: Strong, bitter
Form: Whole or powdered roots, cut leaves
Uses: Tea
Home garden: Outdoors

Goldenrod

Blue Mountain tea
Solidago species
Origin: United States
Parts: Flowering tops, leaves
Flavor: Mild
Form: Cut
Uses: Dye, tea, decoration
Home garden: Outdoors

Goldenseal

Hydrastis canadensis
Origin: United States
Parts: Roots
Form: Cut, powdered
Uses: Cosmetics
Home garden: Not recommended

Great mullein

Aaron's rod
Verbascum thapsus
Origin: Europe, Asia
Parts: Leaves, flowers
Flavor: Mild
Form: Cut
Uses: Tea
Home garden: Outdoors

Henna

Lawsonia inermis
Origin: North Africa, Asia, Australia
Parts: Leaves, flowers
Form: Cut or ground
Uses: Fragrance, cosmetics
Home garden: Outdoors as ornamental in warm regions

Hibiscus

Hibiscus rosa-sinensis
Origin: Tropical Asia
Parts: Flowers
Form: Whole
Uses: Tea, dye
Home garden: Indoors/outdoors in warm regions, greenhouse

Hops

Humulus lupulus
Origin: Northern temperate regions
Parts: Female flowers
Flavor: Bitter
Form: Whole
Uses: Beer flavoring
Home garden: Outdoors

Horehound

Marrubium vulgare
Origin: Asia, Europe, North Africa, Azores, Canary Islands
Parts: Leaves
Flavor: Bitter
Form: Cut
Uses: Tea, candy
Home garden: Outdoors

Horseradish

Armoracia rusticana
Origin: Southeast Europe
Parts: Fleshy roots
Flavor: Hot, pungent
Form: Powdered
Uses: Culinary
Home garden: Outdoors

Hyssop

Hyssopus officinalis
Origin: Europe
Parts: Leaves, flowers
Form: Cut
Uses: Fragrance, decoration
Home garden: Outdoors

Indigo, false

Wild indigo, horsefly
Baptisia tinctoria
Origin: United States
Parts: Leaves, pods, bark
Form: Cut
Uses: Dye
Home garden: Outdoors

Jasmine

Jasminum species
Origin: Asia, Africa, Australia
Parts: Flowers
Scent: Sweet
Form: Petals
Uses: Tea, fragrance
Home garden: Indoors/outdoors in warm regions

Juniper

Juniperus communis
Origin: North America, Eurasia
Parts: Berrylike cones
Flavor: Slightly bitter
Form: Whole
Uses: Culinary, gin flavoring, fragrance, dye
Home garden: Outdoors

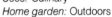

Kava-kava

Piper methysticum
Origin: Pacific Islands
Parts: Roots
Flavor: Bitter
Form: Ground
Uses: Beverage
Home garden: Not recommended

Kelp

Seaweed
Macrosytica pyrifera (Atlantic) and *Fucus versiculosus* (Pacific)
Origin: Oceans
Parts: Foliage
Flavor: Mild to bitter
Form: Cut
Uses: Culinary
Home garden: Not recommended

Lady's mantle

Alchemilla vulgaris
Origin: Europe
Parts: Leaves
Form: Cut
Uses: Fragrance, cosmetics
Home garden: Indoors/outdoors

Lavender

Lavandula species
Origin: Europe
Parts: Leaves, blossoms
Form: Whole, cut
Uses: Fragrance, decoration
Home garden: Indoors/outdoors

Lemon balm

Melissa officinalis
Origin: Southern France
Parts: Leaves
Flavor: Lemonlike
Form: Crushed
Uses: Culinary, tea, cosmetics, fragrance
Home garden: Indoors, outdoors except in very hot regions

Lemongrass

Oil grass, West Indian lemongrass, fever grass
Cymbopogon citratus
Origin: India, Ceylon
Parts: Leaves, stems
Flavor: Lemonlike
Form: Cut
Uses: Tea, fragrance
Home garden: Not recommended

Lemon verbena
Aloysia triphylla
Origin: Argentina, Chile
Parts: Leaves
Flavor: Lemonlike
Form: Cut
Uses: Culinary, fragrance, tea
Home garden: Indoors, greenhouse, or outdoors in very mild climates

Licorice
Glycyrrhiza glabra
Origin: Mediterranean, Asia
Parts: Roots
Flavor: Distinctive
Form: Sticks, pieces, powdered
Uses: Culinary, fragrance
Home garden: Outdoors

Lily-of-the-valley
Convallaria majalis
Origin: Europe
Parts: Leaves, flowers
Form: Cut
Uses: Dye (leaves), fragrance (flowers)
Home garden: Outdoors, greenhouse

Linden
Tilia species
Origin: Northern temperate zones
Parts: Flowers
Flavor: Mild
Form: Whole
Uses: Cosmetics, fragrance
Home garden: Outdoors

Lotus
Nelumbo species
Origin: Asia, North America
Parts: Roots
Flavor: Subtle
Form: Sliced
Uses: Culinary
Home garden: Water gardens

Lovage
Levisticum officinale
Origin: Southern Europe
Parts: Seeds, stalks, leaves
Flavor: Celerylike
Form: Cut leaves and stalk, whole seed
Uses: Culinary, decoration
Home garden: Outdoors, difficult along warm coasts

Mace
Myristica fragrans
Origin: Moluccas (Indonesia)
Parts: Seed coverings only (aril)
Flavor: Strong nutmeg
Form: Blades, ground
Uses: Culinary, fragrance
Home garden: Not recommended

Madder
Rubia tinctorum
Origin: Southern Europe, Asia Minor
Parts: Roots
Form: Cut
Uses: Dye
Home garden: Outdoors

Malva
Malva sylvestris
Origin: Europe
Parts: Flowers, leaves
Flavor: Delicate
Form: Cut leaves, whole flowers
Uses: Tea, decoration
Home garden: Outdoors

Marjoram
Sweet marjoram
Origanum majorana
Origin: North Africa, Southwest Asia
Parts: Leaves
Flavor: Mild, sweet
Form: Cut
Uses: Culinary
Home garden: Indoors/outdoors

Marsh mallow
Althaea officinalis
Origin: Europe
Parts: Roots, flowers, leaves
Flavor: Mild
Form: Cut leaves and roots, whole flowers
Uses: Tea, decoration
Home garden: Outdoors

Mint
Mentha species
Origin: Europe
Parts: Leaves
Flavor: Distinct, sweet
Form: Cut
Uses: Culinary, fragrance, tea, cosmetics
Home garden: Indoors/outdoors

Mustard
Brassica species
Origin: Europe, Asia
Parts: Seeds
Flavor: Pungent
Form: Whole, powdered
Uses: Culinary
Home garden: Outdoors, weedy

Myrrh
Commiphora myrrha
Origin: North Africa
Parts: Resin
Scent: Sweet, spicy
Form: Gum, powder
Uses: Fragrance
Home garden: Not recommended

Myrtle
Myrtus communis
Origin: Mediterranean
Parts: Leaves
Scent: Spicy
Form: Cut
Uses: Fragrance
Home garden: Outdoors

Nettle

Urtica species

Origin: Europe

Parts: Leaves

Uses: Dye, tea

Home garden: Not recommended

Nutmeg

Myristica fragrans

Origin: Moluccas (Indonesia)

Parts: Peeled seeds

Flavor: Spicy

Form: Whole, ground

Uses: Culinary, fragrance

Home garden: Not recommended

Oat straw

Avena sativa

Origin: Mediterranean

Parts: Stems

Flavor: Mild

Form: Cut

Uses: Tea

Home garden: Not recommended

Onion

Allium cepa

Origin: Northern Hemisphere

Parts: Bulbs

Flavor: Distinct, sweet to strong

Form: Whole, chopped, powdered

Uses: Culinary, dye (skin)

Home garden: Outdoors

Oregano

Wild marjoram, pot marjoram

Origanum vulgare

Origin: Europe, Central Asia

Parts: Leaves

Flavor: Pungent

Form: Cut, powdered

Uses: Culinary, dye

Home garden: Indoors/outdoors

Orris

Florentine iris, German iris

Iris × germanica var. *florentina*

Origin: Probably Mediterranean

Parts: Roots

Scent: Sweet

Form: Pieces, powdered

Uses: Fragrance, cosmetics

Home garden: Outdoors

Papaya

Carica papaya

Origin: Tropical America

Parts: Leaves

Form: Cut

Uses: Soap, cosmetics

Home garden: Outdoors in tropics only

Paprika

Capsicum annuum

Origin: North and South America

Parts: Fruit pods

Flavor: Sweet, spicy

Form: Ground

Uses: Culinary

Home garden: Outdoors

Parsley

Petroselinum crispum

Origin: Europe, Western Asia

Parts: Leaves

Flavor: Mild

Form: Chopped

Uses: Culinary

Home garden: Indoors/outdoors

Passionflower

Passiflora incarnata

Origin: United States

Parts: Leaves, flowers

Flavor: Mild

Form: Cut

Uses: Tea

Home garden: Outdoors

Patchouli

Pogosiemon patchouli

Origin: India, Philippines

Parts: Leaves

Scent: Spicy, strong

Form: cut, ground, powdered

Uses: Fragrance

Home garden: Not recommended

Pennyroyal

Mentha pulegium

Origin: Europe, Western Asia

Parts: Leaves

Flavor: Bitter

Form: Cut

Uses: Cosmetics, tea

Home garden: Indoors, outdoors in mild climates

Pepper

Black pepper (with husk), white pepper (husk removed)

Piper nigrum

Origin: India, Ceylon

Parts: Buds

Flavor: Distinct, hot

Form: Whole, cracked, ground

Uses: Culinary

Home garden: Not recommended

Pimiento

Capsicum annuum

Origin: North and South America

Parts: Fruits

Flavor: Sweet, mild

Form: Whole, chopped

Uses: Culinary

Home garden: Outdoors

Plantain

Plantago major

Origin: Europe, Asia

Parts: Leaves

Form: Cut

Uses: Skin care

Home garden: Not recommended

Pomegranate

Punica granatum
Origin: Europe and
South Asia
Parts: Bark, seeds
Flavor: Tart
Form: Cut bark, whole
seed
Uses: Dye, culinary
(seed)
Home garden: Outdoors
in subtropical climates,
greenhouse

Poppy

Papaver somniferum
Origin: Southeast
Europe, Western Asia
Parts: Seeds
Flavor: Subtle
Form: Whole
Uses: Culinary
Home garden: Illegal in
the United States

Red clover

Trifolium pratense
Origin: Europe
Parts: Flowers
Flavor: Subtle
Form: Whole, cut
Uses: Tea
Home garden: Not
recommended

Redroot

New Jersey tea,
mountain sweet
Ceanothus americanus
Origin: United States
Parts: Roots
Flavor: Subtle
Form: Cut
Uses: Tea, dye
Home garden: Not
recommended

Rose

Rosa species
Origin: Northern
Hemisphere
Parts: Flowers, hips
Flavor: Sweet
Form: Petals cut, hips
whole or crushed
Uses: Culinary, tea,
cosmetics, fragrance,
decoration
Home garden: Outdoors

Rosemary

Rosmarinus officinalis
Origin: Mediterranean
Parts: Leaves, flowers
Flavor: Spicy
Form: Whole, cut,
ground
Uses: Culinary, tea,
cosmetics, fragrance
Home garden:
Indoors/outdoors

Safflower

American saffron, false
saffron
Carthamus tinctorius
Origin: Probably Eurasia
Parts: Flowers
Form: Cut
Uses: Culinary, dye,
cosmetics, decoration
Home garden:
Ourdoors, best in dry
climates

Saffron

Crocus sativus
Origin: Mediterranean
Parts: Flower stigmas
Flavor: Spicy
Form: Whole strands,
ground
Uses: Culinary, dye
Home garden: Outdoors

Sage

Salvia species
Origin: Worldwide
Parts: Leaves
Flavor: Strong
Form: Cut, ground
Uses: Culinary, tea,
fragrance, dye,
decoration
Home garden:
Indoors/outdoors

Sandalwood

Santalum album
Origin: India
Parts: Wood
Form: Chips, powdered
Uses: Fragrance
Home garden: Not
recommended

Sarsaparilla

Smilax species
Origin: Tropical America
Parts: Roots
Form: Cut, powdered
Uses: Culinary,
fragrance
Home garden: Not
recomrnended

Sassafras

Sassafras albidum
Origin: United States
Parts: Bark, young
leaves
Flavor: Rootbeerlike
Form: Cut, powdered
Uses: Culinary,
fragrance, tea
Home garden: Outdoors

Savory

Satureja species
Origin: Mediterranean
Parts: Leaves
Flavor: Tangy (winter),
sweet (summer)
Form: Cut
Uses: Culinary
Home garden:
Indoors/outdoors

Sesame

Benne
Sesamum indicum
Origin: Tropics
Parts: Seeds
Flavor: Nutty
Form: Whole
Uses: Culinary
Home garden: Outdoors
in warm climates

Shallot

Allium cepa
Origin: Northern
Hemisphere
Parts: Bulbs
Flavor: Delicate
onionlike
Form: Whole, diced
Uses: Culinary
Home garden: Outdoors

Soapwort
Saponaria officinalis
Origin: Europe, Asia
Parts: Roots
Form: Cut
Uses: Soap substitute, cosmetics
Home garden: Not recommended

Southernwood
Old-man
Artemisia abrotanum
Origin: Southern Europe
Parts: Leaves
Scent: Strong
Form: Cut
Uses: Fragrance, decoration
Home garden: Outdoors

Speedwell
St. Paul's betony, gypsyweed
Veronica officinalis
Origin: Europe, Asia, North America
Parts: Leaves
Form: Cut
Uses: Tea
Home garden: Outdoors

St.-John's-wort
Hypericum species
Origin: Temperate zones
Parts: Blooming tops
Form: Cut
Uses: Cosmetics, dye
Home garden: Outdoors

Star anise
Illiciurn verum
Origin: China, Vietnam
Parts: Unripe fruits, bark
Flavor: Spicy
Form: Whole, chips
Uses: Culinary, fragrance
Home garden: Outdoors in warm climates

Strawberry
Woodland strawberry
Fragaria vesca
Origin: Eurasia, North America
Parts: Leaves
Flavor: Mild
Form: Cut
Uses: Tea
Home garden: Outdoors

Sumac
Smooth sumac
Rhus glabra
Origin: North America
Parts: Berries, roots, leaves
Form: Whole berries, cut roots, and leaves
Uses: Dye, decoration
Home garden: Outdoors

Sunflower
Helianthus annuus
Origin: North America
Parts: Seeds, flower petals
Flavor: Nutty
Form: Whole
Uses: Culinary, dye
Home garden: Outdoors

Sweet flag
Calamus
Acorus calamus
Origin: Northern Hemisphere
Parts: Roots
Scent: Sweet
Form: Cut, powdered
Uses: Fragrance
Home garden: Outdoors water garden

Tabasco
Capsicum frutescens
Origin: Tropical America
Parts: Fruits
Flavor: Hot
Form: Liquid sauce
Uses: Culinary
Home garden: Not recommended

Tansy
Tanacetum vulgare
Origin: Europe, Asia
Parts: Leaves, flowers
Form: Cut
Uses: Cosmetics, dye, decoration
Home garden: Outdoors

Tarragon
Estragon
Artemisia dracunculus
Origin: Southern Europe, Asia, Western United States
Parts: Leaves
Flavor: Sweet
Form: Cut
Uses: Culinary
Home garden: Indoors/outdoors

Tea
Black, green, or Oolong
Camellia sinensis
Origin: Asia
Parts: Leaves
Flavor: Distinct, aromatic
Form: Cut
Uses: Tea
Home garden: Outdoors or greenhouse as ornamental

Thyme
Thymus species
Origin: Europe, Asia
Parts: Leaves
Flavor: Slightly pungent
Form: Cut
Uses: Culinary, tea, fragrance
Home garden: Indoors/outdoors

Turmeric
Curcuma domestica
Origin: Tropical Asia
Parts: Tuberous rhizomes
Flavor: Subtle
Form: Powdered
Uses: Culinary, dye
Home garden: Outdoors in warm climates, greenhouse

Valerian

Allheal, garden heliotrope, phew plant
Valeriana officinalis
Origin: Europe, Western Asia
Parts: Roots
Form: Cut, powdered
Uses: Cosmetics
Home garden: Outdoors

Vanilla

Vanilla planifolia
Origin: Tropical America
Parts: Seed pods
Flavor: Unique, aromatic
Form: Whole, powdered, liquid extract
Uses: Culinary, fragrance
Home garden: Greenhouse as ornamental

Vervain

Verbena species
Origin: Tropical America
Parts: Leaves
Flavor: Strong
Form: Cut
Uses: Tea
Home garden: Outdoors

Violet

Viola odorata
Origin: Europe, Africa, Asia
Parts: Flowers, leaves
Fragrance: Sweet
Form: Cut leaves, whole or candied flowers
Uses: Culinary, tea, fragrance, cosmetics, decoration
Home garden: Outdoors

Water chestnut

Eleocharis dulcis
Origin: Tropical Asia, Pacific Islands, Madagascar, West Africa
Parts: Tubers or corms
Flavor: Subtle
Form: Whole
Uses: Culinary
Home garden: Outdoor water garden

Watercress

Nasturtium officinale
Origin: Europe
Parts: Leaves and stems
Flavor: Slightly peppery
Form: Cut
Uses: Culinary
Home garden: Outdoor water garden

Wasabi

Japanese horseradish
Wasabia japonica
Origin: Asia
Parts: Roots
Flavor: Very hot, pungent
Form: Powdered
Uses: Culinary
Home garden: Not recommended

Wintergreen

Teaberry, checkerberry, mountain tea
Gaultheria procumbens
Origin: United States
Parts: Leaves
Flavor: Minty
Form: Cut
Uses: Culinary, tea, cosmetics, fragrance
Home garden: Not recommended

Witch hazel

Hamamelis virginiana
Origin: Eastern North America
Parts: Leaves, bark
Form: Cut
Uses: Cosmetics
Home garden: Outdoors

Wood betony

Bishop's wort, woundwort
Stachys officinalis
Origin: Europe, Asia
Parts: Leaves, flowers
Scent: Strong, minty
Form: Cut
Uses: Tea, decoration
Home garden: Outdoors

Woodruff

Sweet woodruff
Galium odoratum
Origin: Europe, North Africa, Asia
Parts: Leaves
Scent: Sweet
Form: Cut
Uses: Culinary, tea, fragrance
Home garden: Indoors/outdoors

Wormwood

Artemisia absinthium
Origin: Europe
Parts: Leaves
Fragrance: Strong, spicy
Form: Cut
Uses: Fragrance, insect repellent, decoration, beverage flavoring
Home garden: Toxic, not recommended

Yarrow

Achillea millefolium
Origin: Europe, Western Asia
Parts: Leaves, flowers
Scent: Strong
Form: Cut
Uses: Cosmetics, dye, decoration
Home garden: Outdoors

Yellow dock

Rumex crispus
Origin: Europe, North and South America
Parts: Roots (flowers dried for decoration)
Form: Cut
Uses: Dye
Home garden: Not recommended

Yerba maté

Maté, Paraguay tea
Ilex paraguariensis
Origin: South America
Parts: Leaves
Flavor: Strong
Form: Cut
Uses: Tea
Home garden: Not recommended

Directory of Common Herb Names

Use this listing to look up botanical counterparts of most of the common names used in the text. Refer to the index or the Plant Selection Guide to locate specific information on each plant.

A sweet herbal harvest yields pomanders, teas, and flavorings.

Agrimony: *Agrimonia eupatoria*
Ajuga: *Ajuga reptans*
Alfalfa: *Medicago sativa*
Alkanet: *Anchusa officinalis*
Allspice: *Pimenta dioica*
Aloe or aloe vera: *Aloe barbadensis*
Angelica: *Angelica* species
Anise: *Pimpinella anisum*
Annatto: *Bixa orellana*
Arrowroot: *Maranta arundinacea*
Artemisia: *Artemisia* species
Asparagus: *Asparagus officinalis*
Barberry: *Berberis vulgaris*
Basil: *Ocimum basilicum*
Bay: *Laurus nobilis*
Bayberry: *Myrica pensylvanica*
Bedstraw: *Galium verum*
Bee balm: *Monarda didyma*
Bergamot: *Monarda* species
Birch: *Betula* species
Blackberry: *Rubus* species
Bloodroot: *Sanguinaria canadensis*
Boneset: *Eupatorium perfoliatum*
Borage: *Borago officinalis*
Boxwood: *Buxus* species
Burdock: *Arctium lappa*
Burnet: *Poterium sanguisorba*
Calendula: *Calendula officinalis*
Capers: *Capparis spinosa*
Caraway: *Carum carvi*
Cardamom: *Elettaria cardamomum*
Carnation: *Dianthus caryophyllus*
Carob: *Ceratonia siliqua*
Catnip: *Nepeta cataria*
Cayenne: *Capsicum annuum*
Cedar, red: *Juniperus virginiana*
Celery: *Apium graveolens*
Chamomile: *Chamaemelum nobile*
Chervil: *Anthriscus cerefolium*
Chia: *Salvia columbariae*
Chicory: *Cichorium intybus*
Chili pepper: *Capsicum annuum*
Chives: *Allium schoenoprasum*
Chives, Chinese: *Allium tuberosum*
Chocolate: *Theobroma cacao*
Chrysanthemum, garland: *Chrysanthemum coronarium*
Cilantro: *Coriandrum sativum*
Cinnamon: *Cinnamomum zeylanicum*
Cinnamon, Chinese: *Cinnamomum cassia*
Citrus: *Citrus* species
Cloves: *Syzygium aromaticum*
Coffee: *Coffea arabica*
Cola nut: *Cola acuminata*
Coltsfoot: *Tussilago farfara*
Comfrey: *Symphytum officinale*
Coriander: *Coriandrum sativum*
Cornflower: *Centaurea cyanus*
Costmary: *Chrysanthemum balsamita*
Cowslip: *Primula veris*
Cubeb: *Piper cubeba*
Cumin: *Cuminum cyminum*
Damiana: *Turnera aphrodisiaca*
Dandelion: *Taraxacum officinale*
Desert tea: *Ephedra* species
Dill: *Anethum graveolens*
Dittany of Crete: *Origanum dictamnus*
Dock: *Rumex* species
Dyer's broom: *Genista tinctoria*
Elderberry: *Sambucus canadensis*

Elecampane: *Inula helenium*
Eucalyptus: *Eucalyptus* species
Fennel: *Foeniculum vulgare*
Fennel flower: *Nigella sativa*
Fenugreek: *Trigonella foenum-graecum*
Foxglove: *Digitalis purpurea*
Frankincense: *Boswellia* species
Fumitory: *Fumaria officinalis*
Garlic: *Allium sativum*
Gas Plant: *Dictamnus albus*
Geraniums, scented: *Pelargonium* species
Germander: *Teucrium chamaedrys*
Ginger: *Zingiber officinale*
Ginseng: *Panax quinquefolius*
Goldenrod: *Solidago odora*
Goldenseal: *Hydrastis canadensis*
Good-King-Henry: *Chenopodium bonus-henricus*
Great mullein: *Verbascum thapsus*
Heliotrope: *Heliotropium arborescens*
Hen-and-chickens: *Sempervivum* species
Henna: *Lawsonia inermis*
Hibiscus: *Hibiscus rosa-sinensis*
Hollyhock: *Alcea rosea*
Hops: *Humulus lupulus*
Horehound: *Marrubium vulgare*
Horseradish: *Armoracia rusticana*
Hyssop: *Hyssopus officinalis*
Indigo, false or wild: *Baptisia tinctoria*
Jasmine: *Jasminum* species
Johnny-jump-up: *Viola tricolor*
Juniper: *Juniperus communis*
Kava-kava: *Piper methysticum*
Kelp (Atlantic): *Macrosytica pyrifera*
Kelp (Pacific): *Fucus versiculosus*
Lady's mantle: *Alchemilla vulgaris*
Lamb's ears: *Stachys byzantina*
Lavender: *Lavandula* species
Leek: *Allium ampeloprasum*
Lemon balm: *Melissa officinalis*
Lemon verbena: *Aloysia triphylla*
Lemongrass: *Cymbopogon citratus*
Licorice: *Glycyrrhiza glabra*
Lily-of-the-valley: *Convallaria majalis*
Linden: *Tilia* species
Lotus: *Nelumbo* species
Lovage: *Levisticum officinale*
Mace: *Myristica fragrans*
Madder: *Rubia tinctorum*
Malva: *Malva sylvestris*
Marjoram: *Origanum majorana*
Marsh mallow: *Althaea officinalis*
Mint: *Mentha* species
Mustard: *Brassica* species
Myrrh: *Commiphora myrrha*
Myrtle: *Myrtus communis*
Nasturtium: *Tropaeolum* species
Nettle: *Urtica* species
Nutmeg: *Myristica fragrans*
Oat straw: *Avena sativa*
Onion: *Allium cepa*
Oregano: *Origanum vulgare*
Orris: *Iris* × *germanica* var. *florentina*
Papaya: *Carica papaya*
Paprika: *Capsicum annuum*
Parsley: *Petroselinum crispum*
Passionflower: *Passiflora incarnata*
Patchouli: *Pogosiemon patchouli*
Pennyroyal: *Mentha pulegium*
Pepper: *Piper nigrum; Capsicum* species

Pimiento: *Capsicum annuum*
Pink: *Dianthus* species
Plantain: *Plantago major*
Pomegranate: *Punica granatum*
Poppy: *Papaver somniferum*
Red clover: *Trifolium pratense*
Redroot: *Ceanothus americanus*
Rocket: *Eruca vesicaria* subspecies *sativa*
Rose: *Rosa* species
Rosemary: *Rosmarinus officinalis*
Rue: *Ruta graveolens*
Safflower: *Carthamus tinctorius*
Saffron: *Crocus sativus*
Sage: *Salvia* species
St.-John's-wort: *Hypericum* species
Sandalwood: *Santalum album*
Santolina: *Santolina* species
Sarsaparilla: *Smilax* species
Sassafras: *Sassafras albidum*
Savory: *Satureja* species
Sesame: *Sesamum indicum*
Shallot: *Allium cepa*
Shisho: *Perilla frutescens* 'Crispa'
Soapwort: *Saponaria officinalis*
Sorrel: *Rumex* species
Southernwood: *Artemisia abrotanum*
Speedwell: *Veronica officinalis*
Star anise: *Illicium verum*
Strawberry: *Fragaria vesca*
Sumac: *Rhus glabra*
Sunflower: *Helianthus annuus*
Sweet cicely: *Myrrhis odorata*
Sweet flag: *Acorus calamus*
Sweet olive: *Osmanthus fragrans*
Tabasco: *Capsicum frutescens*
Tansy: *Tanacetum vulgare*
Tarragon: *Artemisia dracunculus*
Tea: *Camellia sinensis*
Thyme: *Thymus* species
Turmeric: *Curcuma domestica*
Valerian: *Valeriana officinalis*
Vanilla: *Vanilla planifolia*
Vervain: *Verbena canadensis*
Violet: *Viola odorata*
Wasabi: *Wasabia japonica*
Water chestnut: *Eleocharis dulcis*
Watercress: *Nasturtium officinale*
Wintergreen: *Gaultheria procumbens*
Witch hazel: *Hamamelis virginiana*
Wood betony: *Stachys officinalis*
Woodruff: *Galium odoratum*
Wormwood: *Artemisia absinthium*
Yarrow: *Achillea millefolium*
Yellow dock: *Rumex crispus*
Yerba maté: *Ilex paraguariensis*

Sources

Mail-Order Plants and Seeds

In addition to the herb specialists listed below, most of the major vegetable and flower seed companies offer common herbs in their garden catalogs. There may be a charge for the catalogs.

Carpilands Herb Farm
Silver Street
Coventry, CT 06238

Carroll Gardens
P.O. Box 310
Westminster, MD 21157

Fox Hill Farm
Box 7
Parma, MN 49269
Open April 15 through October 1.

Greene Herb Gardens
Greene, RI 02827

Hemlock Hill Herb Farm
Litchfield, CT 06759
Plants only.

Herbitage Farms
Old Homestead Highway
RFD 2
Richmond, NH 03470

Kitazawa Seed Co.
356 W. Taylor Street
San Jose, CA 95110

Logee's Greenhouses
55 North Street
Danielson, CT 06239

Merry Gardens
Camden, ME 04843

Mincemoyer Nursery
1190 N. Pacific Highway
Albany, OR 97321

Nichol's Garden Nursery
1190 N. Pacific Highway
Albany, OR 97321

Otto Richter and Sons, Ltd.
Goodwood, Ontario
LOC 1AO Canada

Clyde Robin Seed Co.
Box 2855
Castro Valley, CA 94546

Roses of Yesterday and Today
802 Brown's Valley Road
Watsonville, CA 95076
Rose plants only.

Savage Farm Nursery
Box 125
McMinnville, TN 37110

Taylor's Herb Gardens, Inc.
1535 Lone Oak Road
Vista, CA 92083
Plants only.

Index

Italicized page numbers refer to illustrations. Common names are cross-referenced to botanical names on page 141.